A
PERFECT
CHILDHOOD

Growing Up in the 1960s with
Baseball, The Beatles, and Beaver Cleaver

GARY D'AMATO

PathBinder
Publishing LLC
COLUMBUS, INDIANA

2023

Published by PathBinder Publishing
P.O. Box 2611
Columbus, IN 47202 www.PathBinderPublishing.com

*Cover images submitted by Gary D'Amato,
except baseball image by Pixabay
Front and back covers designed by Anna Perlich*

First published in 2020
Manufactured in the United States

ISBN 978-1-955088-66-4

For my parents, Peter and Nancy. From my dad, I inherited a love for sports; from my mom, a love for writing. A half-century later, I'm still writing about sports.

Also, for my long-ago friends on Bolivar and Whittaker avenues in St. Francis, Wisconsin, many of them mentioned in this book: John Kresl, Peter Markiewicz, Frank Mahuta, Clark Chiaverotti, Butch and Mike Derrick, Bob Koehler, Mike Counihan, Greg and Wayne Zigoy, Henry Brazil, Mike Rudolph, Jim Tatera, Jeff and Greg Laskowski, David Tarnowski and Jim Forster. We had some great times, didn't we?

FORWARD

It was through our mutually beloved and late friend, Chuck Sindorf, that I first met Gary D'Amato over a quarter century ago. Gary was the golf writer for the *Milwaukee Journal Sentinel* (where Chuck also worked) and I was competing in the Wisconsin amateur golf circuit.

Gary, a respected journalist, could easily coax me, a self-absorbed tournament player, into some gratuitous cock-of-the-walk commentary on many of golf's issues du jour, be it the superhero sensation I enjoyed when surveying planet earth from the precipice of certain elevated tee boxes, or my opinion on an outrageous mid-nineties metal group known as the Ping Zing 2 Irons, or even rating the redemption qualities found in post-round public course grillroom burgers across southeastern Wisconsin (including rating the ratings of other burger raters). I would talk, and Gary, the writer, would listen, unfailingly tolerant and kind.

It's what he does and who he is.

But that's only a part of what he does and who he is.

It is common knowledge that Gary is first and foremost, a listener. He's a prober, a discerner, and a nonstop learner. A prose pro and an author of several books (including the one in your hands, be it on paper or electronic). He's also a many time state and national award-winner for golf and sports writing in multiple categories. He has covered the world's most important sporting events in faraway lands as well as decidedly smaller events closer to home featuring the efforts of local heroes written from the comfort of his own swag-stuffed home office.

But whatever the event or who the subject, Gary D has had a knack for sidestepping any tedium to find a bona fide story. Stories that inform, entertain, and often enlighten by way of Gary's knowing and wry-at-times take on what others have attempted or achieved or suffered through or overcome (or a combination thereof) in competition.

All with a wily eye for all that goes into the preparation and the often profound context that makes competition and rivalries and the kind of personal global brand expansion that seeks to shod half the world with Nike Air Costanzas (or whatever) so compelling.

As our friendship grew, I discovered there was a side to Gary that I found fascinating, but few others knew about. Maybe it's more a dimension to him than a side. A side is an order of fries; a dimension skews closer to core values.

Net-net, Gary is a player.

He may be among the best ever in our state to bring us stories on the achievements and the inner essence of others, including some of the world's greatest athletes. But, so too does Gary choose to compete in his own right. He does so by being a quietly ferocious participator in life … an undercover grinder in the best sense. In fact, it would be fair to say that Gary is among the most "for the love of the game" guys I've ever known, observed, or read about. Frankly, there happens to be a lot of stuff more people should know about Gary D'Amato.

Prima facie: Since 1975, Gary has participated in a regular tag football game from 9 a.m. to noon, every Saturday from Labor Day through Super Bowl Sunday. The only justifiable reason for cancellation is when the wind-chill fails to reach at least 20 degrees *below zero*. It's only happened a few times in 45 years. Otherwise, the game goes on. It might be in excess of 90 degrees, could be blizzardy with thigh-high snow, or treacherous with monsoon-infused mud baths. Doesn't matter. Game on.

Like the Jackson 5's hometown on Lake Michigan with whom he shares a name, Gary's there. And he was there to play, mind-bogglingly, soon after the events that took place in the early morning hours of August 30, 2003. Gary was bicycling back to his home in Caledonia, Wisconsin, after attending Harley-Davidson's 100-year anniversary celebration in Milwaukee. (Hey, what's 20 miles each way?) A delivery truck cruised through a flashing red light on Kinnickinnic Avenue and barreled smack into Gary. He suffered a torn PCL, a torn MCL, a compound fracture, and shredded biceps tendon, while ruining more soft tissues than Nicholas Sparks.

Yet, with a leg immobilized in a brace and virtually useless, he returned to play a mere two months later. (This pops into my mind whenever Milwaukee Brewers outfielder Ryan Braun is scratched from the lineup after tweaking something tightening a batting glove).

"I could only play quarterback and I played poorly," was how Gary put it.

There's no doubt Lawrence Taylor's infamous leg-fracturing hit on Joe Theismann had to really hurt. But I'm pretty sure a delivery truck turning into a middle-aged biker on a concrete street has got to be worse, and probably rises to the level of atrocity. At least Ben Hogan had a Cadillac around him when a Greyhound bus plowed head-on into the famed golfer in 1949.

But the game goes on in Gary's world. He enters the fall of the 2020 tag football season for his 46th year, having participated in more than 600 games … about twice Brett Favre's career games-played total.

Blind in one eye since birth, Gary struggled to hit certain pitches – mostly anything thrown overhand – yet he played baseball for years in both the over-48- and the 55-and-over Milwaukee Men's Senior Baseball Leagues. We're talking baseball, not softball. He may have been a banjo-hitting utility guy, but he was committed and was part of several city championship teams. One year he had to fill in for the last few innings after the team's second baseman pulled a hammy in the fifth inning of the championship game. The magnitude of the moment reportedly affected the mechanisms regulating not only Gary's breathing, but his digestive and urinary tracts, as well. A small price to pay when the stakes are that high.

The sport he loves most, however, is golf. As has been chronicled in a recent article by Gary himself, he has, utilizing the primitive tools of early upright man (pencil and paper), recorded every single hole of every round he's played over the past 49 years. For the record, his lifetime stats (through May 2020) show he has 711 birdies in 2,622 rounds on 442 golf courses in 26 states and eight countries. But he can get far more granular, as is the way of many C-suite, "can't manage what you can't measure" captains of industry and/or plus-handicap robber barons. Gary is nothing if not insanely precise.

You see, Gary D'Amato is not just a gifted chronicler of other people's exploits, great though he may be at doing that. He is also a doer, a player, a competitor, and a full-blooded participator in life. His new book confirms how all of this was in development throughout his time as a child of the Sixties and then expanded upon as these adventures informed his adulthood. Add up those personal traits and the chosen direction of his life's work and we get this book, *A Perfect Childhood: Growing up in the 1960s with Baseball, The Beatles, and Beaver Cleaver*, a humorously written, nostalgically burnished, and ridiculously relatable collection of true stories curated from Gary D'Amato's life as a kid.

The earnest son of solid parents from St. Francis, Wisconsin, Gary's idiosyncratic tales uniquely capture the universal so effortlessly, one can almost taste the verisimilitude in his words and the ghosts of those he wisely banished. And verisimilitude, of course, makes everything better … not unlike like bacon, butter, and solid ball striking. More simply stated, these vignettes are pure gold, sweetly spun in a way that gilds the laneways leading to our own treasured memories, whether they're of past triumphs or still crush one's personal cringe-o-meter to this day or any of the cheesy goodness in-between.

I wrote earlier how, years ago, Gary was the writer and I was the competitor. Turns out, we've probably always been a bit of both. But Gary D'Amato's influence in my life was such that I've become a more effective listener and ultimately decided to pursue my own fascination with storytelling.

In fact, it was another case of Gary being Gary that inspired me to write my first novel. It was his idea, his push, his sincere faith in my ability, and his encouraging emails that gassed up my engines for every leg of a long ride. Writing. Is. Work.

And so, after 25 years, it is not without at least a wisp of irony that I note that it was Gary who was ultimately voted into the Wisconsin Golf Hall of Fame, not me. Gary earned the honor for his intuitive and tireless coverage of Wisconsin golf for many years, now through *Wisconsin.Golf* after retiring from a much-changed *Journal Sentinel*. But let me assure you that in 2017, our state's entire golf community metaphorically stood together as one and whole-heartedly endorsed the hall of fame induction of Gary D'Amato, a competitor who understands competitors and writes like it.

Now, though, comes something a little different yet delightfully familiar, Gary's latest book, the one you're about to read.

And this one, I can assure you once again, is for everyone.

—John Haines,
Accomplished Wisconsin golfer and author of *Danny Mo*, a golf novel.

PREFACE

I'll start with a confession: I don't know if I had a perfect childhood, but because it's the only childhood I had, that's my story and I'm sticking to it.

I grew up in the 1960s, in an aluminum-sided, 1,200-square-foot, three-bedroom ranch in St. Francis, Wisconsin, a middle-class bedroom suburb of Milwaukee. Nothing distinguished our house from any other house on the block. My father, Pete, a first-generation Italian-American, worked in a factory, and my mother, Nancy, worked for a telephone company. Our collars were definitely blue. We didn't have everything we wanted, but we had everything we needed.

We piled into a white Volkswagen Beetle until Dad finally could afford to buy a used, brown Oldsmobile 88, an enormous tank whose engine once caught fire on the freeway. I attended public schools and Sunday catechism classes at Sacred Heart Catholic church, as did my sister, Linda, and my brother, David. We took lunches to school in brown paper bags. We had home-cooked dinners nearly every night: meat loaf, pork chops, pizza burgers and "simple supper" (mashed potatoes, ground beef and onion soup). We ate as a family with assigned seats around the table.

Our grade school, Willow Glen, was a block away, so when Dad worked second shift at Wisconsin Motors, we could come home for lunch. He made us bologna sandwiches and tomato soup or, on rare occasions, took us to McDonald's, which in the mid-1960s had yet to serve its millionth hamburger (today: "billions and billions served").

We had a dog named Fluffy, until she died from heartworm; the experience was so traumatic that we never again owned another pet, not counting tropical fish or Frisky, a gerbil who gave his life for science (more on that later).

In most ways, I suppose, we were as average as average could be.

Baby boomers growing up in Seattle or New York City or Miami Beach undoubtedly had different experiences, at least from the standpoint of geography and environment. But we all watched *Leave It to Beaver* and *Gilligan's Island*. We all played with G.I. Joes, Barbies (the girls anyway), Slinky and Silly Putty. We all listened to top forty hits on AM radio; in Milwaukee, it was The Mighty 92 WOKY.

Life was simpler back then. Was it better? I'll let others make that determination. All I know is that, on hot summer days, we left the house at eight in the morning and played outside all day, and our parents never worried about us. There was a real sense of community, of neighborhood, of belonging.

People watched out for one another. People cared.

We invented our own fun, used our imaginations, figured things out on our own. We went up and down the block and called for friends until we had enough players for sandlot baseball or kickball games. We managed to pick teams, establish rules, and settle arguments without a single adult present.

When the streetlights came on, we played hide-and-seek or kick the can. We spent our allowances on wax lips, Pez, and Bazooka bubble gum. We rode Schwinn bicycles with banana seats and Topps baseball cards stuck in the spokes (but only the scrubs, like Don Mossi and Mike Hershberger). If there was a signature sound of the '60s other than the Beatles, that was it.

St. Francis had everything a kid could want. My family lived two miles from Lake Michigan, a twenty-minute bus ride from downtown Milwaukee, a three-minute walk from a playground, and half a mile from a swamp teeming with pollywogs and cattails. If we weren't playing pick-up games in streets and alleys, we were launching model rockets in Greene Park or catching air with our bikes on the dilapidated old Leroy bridge or building forts in the swamp.

My block, my neighborhood, and the people who lived in it and the things we did, comprised not only my childhood experiences, but in large part made me who I am today. Five decades later, I look back on those formative years with the wistful longing of a man who understands the priceless value of that time and place and the truth that he can go back only through his memories.

Maybe you feel the same.

I've had fun revisiting my childhood, and introducing you to events and people that I swear are not figments of my imagination. Though you may think it impossible for one boy to experience all that I experienced, or that my extraordinary friends were invented for the sake of storytelling, I assure you everything in these pages happened and that the characters are real people. I may have slightly embellished a few facts on account of nostalgia, as Beaver Cleaver might say, but the stories are ninety-nine percent true.

Perhaps as you read this book, it will spark memories of your own childhood, your forever best friends long forgotten, your die-of-embarrassment moments, and your first halting steps on the shaky bridge from adolescence to adulthood.

The one thing we all have in common is that there is no time quite like the time we had when we were young.

—Gary D'Amato

CONTENTS

Chapter 1

MEET THE BEATLES

In early September 1964, Frank Mahuta and I were playing Strikeout against the steps of his house on Whittaker Avenue when a black stretch limousine with tinted windows slowly drove down the block and stopped in front of us.

Frank committed a balk, momentarily forgetting about Hank Aaron on first base and Mickey Mantle at the plate. We stood still as statues, mouths open, studying the limo as if it were the mothership from *The Day the Earth Stood Still*. Our family car, a Volkswagen Beetle, would have fit in this car's trunk.

The driver's side rear window of the car went down at a steady pace, suggesting it was not being hand-cranked – electric windows! – and a head popped out. Instinctively, Frank and I took a half-step backward. Whoever this was, he was not from the neighborhood.

The head had a mop of dark hair that was in stark contrast to the popular Marine buzz cut of the day. A singsong voice came from somewhere beneath it.

"Hello, boys, can you tell me where Linda D'Amato lives?"

It was the first time I'd ever heard a British accent, not counting television or the movies.

Frank and I stared at each other, dumbfounded. I think the mop head repeated his question as we stood there, bug-eyed and mute. I was eight years old. There was no way I was going to give out my sister's address, which also happened to be my address, to an alien with a British accent. What if he were James Bond? What if there were a hit out on Linda? I think I shook my head. Maybe I croaked out a "No," or maybe Frank did. Maybe we just stood there. I really don't remember.

The window went back up and the limo slowly pulled away.

Frank and I looked at each other and shrugged. Then we went back to our game of Strikeout.

When I got home, I offhandedly told my Mom and Linda about the strange encounter. Linda shrieked and ran to her room, sobbing hysterically. "The Beatles!" she wailed from behind the closed door. "We could have met the Beatles!"

The Beatles? I would have known John Lennon and Paul McCartney if they'd played for the Milwaukee Braves. I'd have been able to tell you their batting averages, too. But I'd only vaguely heard of the Beatles, seeing how I equated pop music with the sub-species also known as girls. A transistor radio was good for one thing: listening to Earl Gillespie call the Braves games on hot summer nights.

Mom explained how, weeks earlier, she had written a letter to The Beatles on behalf of Linda, inviting them to our house for a home-cooked spaghetti dinner when they came to Milwaukee to play a concert. I have no idea how Mom knew where to send the letter, but she was good at that sort of thing. Once, she had written to Dinah Shore, explaining that her toddler son – that would be me – unfailingly ran up to the television screen and kissed it at the beginning of the *Dinah Shore Chevy Show.* A few weeks later, an autographed photo of Ms. Shore arrived in the mail, made out to me and signed,

"Love, Dinah."

If Mom could find Dinah Shore, she could find The Beatles.

She guessed the Fab Four just might want a quiet meal when they landed in Milwaukee, away from the crush of their screaming, fainting, goofy fans. Maybe they'd do it as a publicity stunt. Maybe the idea of breaking bread with an authentic American family in the heartland appealed to their manager. Maybe they liked mostaccioli and meatballs. Who knows?

I do know the following indisputable facts:

- The Beatles did, indeed, play a concert at the Milwaukee Arena on September 4, 1964.

- My mother sent a letter to the group, inviting them to our house for dinner.

- Frank Mahuta and I had a brief encounter with a stretch limousine with tinted windows, out of which popped a head with a mop of dark hair, out of which came a voice with a British accent. *Somebody* was looking for my sister.

I've told the story to dozens of skeptical friends over the years and have gone over the scenario countless times in my mind. Each and every time, I arrive at the same conclusion:

In early September 1964, one of the Beatles actually spoke to me.

If something other than a croaking noise had come out of my mouth, if I'd had the presence of mind to point and say, "One block over, 2901 East Bolivar Avenue," I might have witnessed spaghetti sauce dripping down Ringo Starr's chin or perhaps even heard George Harrison's guitar gently weep.

Hey, Jude, I blew it.

Chapter 2

PINEWOOD DERBY

The coolest thing about being a Cub Scout – cooler than the campouts and the blue uniforms and the solemn oath about obeying the law of the pack – was Pinewood Derby.

If you try to explain it to a non-Scout today, he will look at you as if you have two heads and go back to playing Fortnite. *There was this block of wood, see, and two axles and four tires, and you used your official Cub Scout pocket knife to shape the wood block into a car body, and you painted it and raced it against other kids' cars down an inclined track, and ..."*

Doesn't sound like much fun, does it? But if you were a Cub Scout in the 1960s, Pinewood Derby was your Super Bowl. Every boy wanted to win the blue ribbon, which meant his car was the fastest block of wood on four wheels. Kids gathered around the winning car as if it were an older brother's pirated *Playboy* magazine, whistling in awe as they stroked its lacquered body and spun its wheels. The car's owner bragged about the hours he'd spent carving the wood, applying the paint and lacquer and positioning the decals just so (always one of the keys to victory). All the while, his father, who had done most of the actual work, stood in the background with a smile on his face.

And so it was that I became obsessed with winning the Cub Scout Pack 302 Pinewood Derby. At nine, I had never won anything in my life. I was far from the first kid picked in playground football and baseball games, owing to my scrawny build and Coke-bottle-thick glasses. I was second-seat alto saxophone in the Willow Glen Elementary School band, but Clark Chiaverotti was number one and I couldn't overtake him, no matter how many reeds I went through during cheek-reddening practice sessions.

Pinewood Derby was different. This was something I could win. This was something I *would* win.

I had complete and unshakable faith in my father as the car's designer, builder, and crew chief. My dad could do just about anything. He could throw a baseball so high into the air that it became a tiny white dot against the blue sky. He could whistle so loud we could hear him at the playground nearly a half-mile away. He could say "ring around the collar" in a single belch, an impressive after-dinner trick that never failed to elicit laughs from us kids and a stern "Pete!" from our mother.

When he came home with the Pinewood Derby kit, opened the plastic bag, and spilled the contents onto the kitchen table, I knew I was looking at the winner. All we had to do was put it together.

Over the next few days, I rushed home from school and waited for my dad to come home from work. Then we sat at the table and whittled and carved and whittled and carved, and slowly, the car took shape. When Dad pronounced the bodywork finished, I have to admit I was a bit disappointed. My racer was on the boxy side and looked more like a 1925 Model T than a '65 Mustang. But after we painted it forest green and I applied a number three decal to its nose, it looked a lot faster.

I decided to christen it the Green Hornet, after a popular comic-book hero and TV show. I felt confident for maybe the first time in my life. I just knew the Green Hornet was going to win Cub Scout Pack 302's Pinewood Derby … … until I saw Peter Markiewicz's Blue Bullet.

My hopes were dashed. Peter's car was almost beyond description, an exotic sky blue-and-silver piece of art that looked like a miniature rocket on wheels. The two-tone paint job and smooth, glistening coat of lacquer appeared to be the work of a professional, and the thin, sleek profile of the racer was downright intimidating. Peter's car looked like it could beat the Green Hornet going sideways down the track.

George Markiewicz, Peter's father, was an engineer at a suburban Milwaukee company, Delco Electronics, that built components for the Apollo space program. Mr. Markiewicz could have designed the flush handle for the commode for all I knew, but he was the kind of man whose high forehead seemed to contain more than the standard ration of brains. I imagined that he drew up the plans for the lunar module on his lunch break. I pictured him testing the Blue Bullet in a wind tunnel and giving the thumbs-up to a crew of space program officials holding clipboards and wearing white smocks and serious expressions.

"We must be absolutely certain of the aerodynamics," George Markiewicz would say. "What kind of drag are we seeing at high speed?"

An underling would respond, "There is practically no drag at all, sir. The car is aerodynamically perfect."

Now I was almost embarrassed about my Green Hornet, which suddenly looked clunky and slow. I prepared myself emotionally to accept another stinging defeat, this time at the hands of George and Peter Markiewicz, neither one of whom could throw a spiral nor hit a curve ball, but whose combined IQ was probably about 857.

Pinewood Derby night arrived at Willow Glen, and when the other Cub Scouts got a glimpse of the sleek Blue Bullet, they gathered around Peter and murmured their approval.

The races were head-to-head affairs, with two cars going down the track side-by-side and the winner advancing to the next round. I swelled with pride when the Green Hornet edged Clark's entry, a black painted beauty. Peter's Blue Bullet kept winning, too, and the showdown finally arrived that I wanted with all my heart, but dreaded with all my soul.

Time stood still as we placed our cars at the top of the track. Flushed with excitement, I whispered a prayer, part of me knowing God didn't really care who won Pinewood Derby, but part of me hoping that He knew how desperately I needed to win something, anything, just once.

The Cub Scout leader who doubled as the official Pinewood Derby starter released the lever that started the cars down the track. Slowly at first, then gaining speed, they hurtled down the rails. I held my breath, fully expecting to see Peter's Bullet pull away. And then the strangest thing happened. The Hornet got in front by a nose, then a car length, then two lengths. The hairs on the back of my neck stood up as that little block of wood hurtled toward its destiny.

All hell broke loose in Cub Scout Pack 302.

The Hornet had won! Not by inches, but by a figurative mile! I ran down to the end of the track and triumphantly hoisted her into the air, and the other boys gathered around and pounded me on the back, knocking my glasses askew. Peter picked up the Blue Bullet and examined it with the puzzled, detached look of a scientist wondering how his foolproof experiment had produced such a colossal dud.

I trembled with joy as I accepted the blue ribbon. More than fifty years later, I still haven't won anything that gave me a better feeling than the one I had that night.

I looked over at my dad. He was standing there, arms folded, nodding and grinning from ear to ear.

What I didn't know, and what he later told me, was that he had taken the car axles with him to work at Wisconsin Motors Teledyne and had used a machine to buff them until they were smooth as glass. He explained that it was all about minimizing friction, and the rest was just window dressing. He said he knew the Hornet was ready to rumble when he spun the wheels with his finger and they kept spinning for thirty seconds.

Who needed George Markiewicz's algorithms and wind tunnels?

I had my dad, a factory worker with common sense and an uncommon touch.

I don't know what happened to the Green Hornet or the blue ribbon … stuck in some drawer for years probably and thrown out when I went off to college. But I can still see that little block of wood racing down the track, the memory as fresh and clear as if it happened yesterday.

And when I think of her, and my dad's smile, the hairs stand up on the back of my neck.

Chapter 3

THE THINGS WE DID FOR FUN

Our parents always warned us that if we engaged in certain activities, such as sword fighting with sharpened sticks, "someone is going to lose an eye."

None of us ever did, though my brother, David, came close.

In the 1960s, we were left to our own devices and, outside of school, were rarely supervised by adults. We played on train tracks. We jumped from rooftops holding umbrellas as if they were parachutes. We owned slingshots and jackknives and BB guns. Even if decent helmets made specifically for bicyclists had been widely available (they wouldn't come along until the mid-1970s), we would have had a word for a kid who wore one: sissy.

It's a miracle we made it through our childhoods without weekly visits to the ER.

Would we go back and do it all over again? In a heartbeat.

Here are a few activities we engaged in back then, some of which might be considered dangerous today:

Sharpshooting

When we were in the sixth grade, my best friend John Kresl's parents bought him a BB gun that looked like Marshal Matt Dillon's six-shooter. It was the coolest thing ever. We shot at tin cans and baseball cards (but not stars like Warren Spahn or Roger Maris). We killed G.I. Joe and Gumby dozens of times.

After a while, we grew bored of shooting at inanimate objects. It was time for some live target practice, meaning: me. In retrospect, it probably wasn't a good idea, but what do you expect from a couple of eleven-year-olds with a BB gun?

The idea was that I would pedal as fast as I could on my trusty Schwinn five-speed bike, and as I roared past John's house, he would try to wing me. I figured my odds of survival were pretty good. It was a thirty-yard shot at a moving object, and it was nighttime. Not even John Wayne could have hit me.

Apparently, John Kresl was a better shot than the Duke.

I was pedaling like a madman and thought I was in the clear when it felt like someone whacked me in the side of the head with a baseball bat. The BB hit me in the forehead, an inch above my right eye. It stung like hell, but somehow, I stayed upright on my bike.

Since I was legally blind in my left eye from birth, the shot could have been catastrophic had it hit my good eye. But, hey, no one ever accused us of having an overabundance of common sense.

Rug Divot

The golf bug bit me hard when I was fourteen, and one night while my parents were out, I decided to practice my swing in the living room. Things were going great until I took a healthy cut with my pitching wedge and watched in horror as a piece of carpet literally flew across the room.

I looked down and was staring at a perfect divot hole, three inches wide by five inches long. The wooden floor beneath was exposed. Arnold Palmer would have been proud. Unfortunately, my father's name was Peter D'Amato.

Breaking out in a cold sweat, I moved a throw rug over the offending hole. But this wasn't something I could hide forever. It was much worse than a broken window or a scratch in the car door or even a giant whitehead on the tip of my nose on class picture day.

When my parents came home from wherever they were, I ran to the door and pleaded, "Please don't kill me! Please don't kill me!" Thinking I'd maimed my younger brother, David, they rushed past me in a panic.

They probably were so relieved that David still had all of his limbs attached that when I pulled back the throw rug to expose the hole in the carpet, they were remarkably calm. Even my dad, who had a volcanic Italian temper – an oxymoron if ever there was one – took it pretty much in stride. As it turned out, the carpet was almost ten years old and they were planning to replace it anyway.

After that, I still practiced golf in the house. But only with my putter.

Killing the Tide Box

Don't ask me why I was repeatedly stabbing an empty Tide laundry detergent box with a dart in the basement. There is no explanation, other than that I was a garden variety clueless kid.

Anyhow, as I stabbed harder and harder, carelessly holding the box in my left hand, I somehow stabbed my index finger, the dart going clean through the fleshy part just under the bone between the first and second knuckles.

It happened so fast that I didn't feel any pain. Well, not initially anyway.

I ran upstairs, the dart sticking completely through my finger, and our babysitter, Diane Szukalski, nearly fainted. Thinking quickly but maybe not clearly, she grabbed the dart and yanked it out. Thankfully, the puncture wound barely bled, and I did not develop gangrene.

Now you know why laundry detergent is sold in plastic bottles.

Firestarter

Around the age of ten, I developed a short-lived and unhealthy fascination with fire. I did not grow up to be an arsonist, thank God, which I attribute to the sheer terror that gripped me when I almost burned down our house.

Since both of my parents smoked at the time, there were always matches and lighters lying around. One day, home alone and bored, I was playing with plastic model cars in the basement when I had the brilliant idea to pilfer some lighter fluid from my parents' stash, pour a pool of it on the concrete floor, set it ablaze, and play demolition derby with the cars.

It was fun until things got a bit out of control and the cars started on fire. Panicking, I grabbed a sleeping bag from under the stairwell and threw it over the fire to extinguish it. Instead, the sleeping bag caught fire. I ran to the laundry tub, filled a bucket with water and doused the flames.

The sleeping bag now featured a huge, charred hole. I carefully rolled it up so the hole was not exposed and put it back under the stairwell. I would deal with it later.

The more pressing problem was that the basement was filled with pungent smoke from melted plastic and burned sleeping bag, and my mom would be home from work in thirty minutes.

I opened the basement windows and spent the next half hour flapping the smoke with a towel, trying to get it to disperse. At some point, my sister, Linda, came home, and I enlisted her help and begged her not to rat me out.

I'm sure there was a quid pro quo involved.

When Mom walked through the door, I bolted up the steps and started babbling away, asking her about her day, telling her about mine – but leaving out certain details – and watching her nostrils intently. Did they flare? Did she smell smoke? Miracle of miracles … she did not!

About a year later, my dad was cleaning out the basement stairwell when he came across the charred sleeping bag. He came upstairs with the bag and muttered, "How the hell did this happen?" Some mysteries are better left unsolved.

'His Eye Popped Out"

One day, David and I were playing one-on-one tackle football in the backyard. It wasn't really a fair fight, me being four years older and outweighing him by thirty pounds at the time. I wasn't brave enough to pick on someone my own size, and poor David made for a perfect tackling dummy.

At one point, I face-planted him in the grass, and when he rolled over, one of his eyes appeared to be mangled. A big blob of yellow fatty stuff with veins running through it filled the hole where his eye had been.

Oh, my God! I'd knocked out his eyeball! Not even the bone-jarring tackles of middle linebackers Dick Butkus or Ray Nitschke had ever knocked a running back's eye from its socket.

My dad happened to be in the front yard, trimming bushes. I ran to him yelling, "Dad! Dad! David's eye popped out!"

We ran back to David, still lying in the grass. He blinked a few times and the fatty blob disappeared. Apparently, we all have small fat deposits under our eyelids, and I'd somehow jarred one of his loose. When he blinked, the fatty thing slid back up under his eyelid.

Tackle football, though, was over for the day.

The Weaponizing of Oreos

I'll admit it: I was a mean older brother. I teased my younger brother and sister incessantly. Many was the time David tagged along with me when I went to play with my friends and wound up running home in tears after I'd verbally abused him. How I'd love to go back now and do things differently.

I took it too far, far too often. Once, I was sitting at the kitchen table, having just opened a new bag of Oreo cookies and poured myself a tall glass of milk. Linda was in the kitchen, and I was getting on her about something or other, and it escalated into an argument.

I turned into Don Rickles, hurling insults at her until she ran from the kitchen, crying. A moment later, Mom came running in from the living room.

"I can't take this anymore!" she screamed.

If she'd had a weapon, I might be dead. Instead, she reached for the nearest thing with which to beat me over the head: the newly opened bag of Oreos. She swung that thing like Willie Mays at the plate and pieces of cookies went flying everywhere as I covered up, begging her to stop. It didn't hurt, but man, she was destroying my snack.

When she finished, the bag was empty and the floor was covered with Oreo cookie shards. Calmly, Mom put the empty bag back on the table and walked out of the room.

I set aside my pride, scrambled on all fours, and managed to salvage a few of the bigger pieces of Oreo. But I'd learned a valuable lesson: If you're going to make fun of your sister in the kitchen, hide the cookies.

Speaking of hiding ...

Darryl Staszewski and I had just eaten at the McDonald's on Packard Avenue in Cudahy and were pulling out of the parking lot in my car – a monstrous, purple 1966 Pontiac Bonneville – when I saw Linda drive in with our parents' car. She parked – this was years before the invention of the drive-through window – and went inside.

A light bulb went off. I had the keys to the car in my pocket. Time to prank Linda.

I ran to the car, started it and moved it to the other side of the building. Then I returned to my car and we waited, giggling. Linda emerged with her bag of food and walked to where she'd parked the car. She stood there frozen, looking at the empty space. She looked left and right, left and right.

Thirty seconds passed. A minute. The look on her face was priceless.

Both of us started crying, but in my case, it was because I was laughing so hard.

Finally, just as she was about to go back into McDonald's to call the police – or worse, our Dad – I ran up to her and, still laughing, half-heartedly apologized. She failed to see the humor in it.

It's a good thing Mom wasn't around with a bag of Oreos.

Chapter 4

PETER THE WHIZ KID

Our family moved into a new three-bedroom ranch house on Bolivar Avenue in St. Francis in January 1962. That winter was cold and dark and lonely, and by late springtime, I still hadn't made any friends. Sure, I'd gotten to know a few kids at Willow Glen Elementary School, but we went our separate ways when the bell rang. You can only play with Army men alone in your bedroom for so long.

One Sunday, when we returned home from church and Dad turned into the alley to park the car, I noticed a boy about my age standing still as a statue in a small field behind a neighbor's house.

"Why don't you go introduce yourself?" my mom said.

Summoning all the courage a six-year-old could muster, I approached the boy, who still hadn't moved a muscle. I noticed he had a glass jar in one hand and the lid in the other. "Hi," I said. "What are you doing?" "Catching bees," he said.

"What for?"

"To study them."

Naturally, this begged a question.

"Do you ever get stung?" I asked.

"Yes, once in a while," he said, "but I've developed a tolerance and … OWWW!"

And that was how I met Peter Markiewicz, who would become one of my best friends through grade school. Peter was different than the rest of us, but I attributed that to his extraordinarily high IQ. Some kids can hit a curve ball, some can ride a skateboard or pop a wheelie, and the rare few can talk to members of the opposite sex (in our case, girls) without stammering. Peter's gift was a heaping helping of brain cells. He was the smartest kid in St. Francis, and number two wasn't close. By the time we were in the sixth grade, Peter could have taught science class. No offense, Mr. Holson.

Because Peter operated on a different wavelength and was inclined to turn the other cheek, it was inevitable that he would be teased and taunted. He was subjected almost daily to playground wisecracks – *"Hey, here comes Monkey-tits"* – but Peter was unflappable. Invariably, he came back with calm retorts that befuddled his tormentors, mainly because they didn't understand a word he said.

On a few occasions, the bullying went to DEFCON 4. When we were in the eighth grade, Peter left his street shoes on the floor outside his locker during gym class, and when he returned to shower, he found one of the shoes filled to the top with urine.

That made for a very unpleasant after-school period in Mr. Goelz's class. The girls were dismissed at the bell after a thorough investigation determined none of them could possibly be the perp, seeing as how they had the wrong set of chromosomes. It was just us boys now squirming in our desks and waiting for the other shoe to drop, so to speak. Mr. Goelz, an imposing man with a booming baritone and a trick knee, growled, "We're going to stay here until I find out who took a whiz in Markiewicz's shoe!"

This was serious business, and Mr. Goelz was not to be trifled with … but have you ever heard a better line? We walked around for weeks afterward, lowering our voices and asking each other conspiratorially, "Who took a whiz in Markiewicz's shoe?"

Of course, no one stepped forward. Who volunteers for a death sentence? The minutes ticked by in silence. Mr. Goelz sat at his desk and stared at us with dark, smoldering eyes. Neither side was going to cave, one out of anger, the other out of fear. I surveyed the room trying to figure out who could have done the dastardly deed. I had my suspicions, but there was no way the culprit was going to confess now.

An hour went by. Our parents had to be wondering who'd kidnapped the entire eighth-grade class of boys at Willow Glen. Soon, the St. Francis police would be called in to examine the crime scene. We were scared, but we were also bored. Jeff Kaja, sitting behind me near the back of the classroom, fashioned a miniature bow-and-arrow from a rubber band and a pencil. Grinning maniacally, he was removing the innards from Bic pens and surreptitiously launching them into the soft ceiling tiles above us. Some of them stuck, quivering for a minute or two, before falling back to the floor.

This was getting surreal.

Finally, Mr. Goelz had no choice but to grudgingly dismiss us. We'd pissed away, if you'll pardon the expression, the better part of two hours. I never did find out who took a whiz in Markiewicz's shoe. As far as I know, the criminal is still out there somewhere, holding his breath, waiting for the statute of limitations to expire.

That summer, one bully actually challenged Peter to a fistfight. Six or seven of us gathered around the combatants, and Dave "Fig" Newton served as referee, laying down the ground rules. I was worried for Peter, but too afraid to intervene and risk getting my nose bloodied, too.

The other kid assumed a boxing stance and started circling Peter, who stood perfectly erect and as still as the day I'd met him in that field catching bees.

And then the damnedest thing happened.

Whack. Peter flicked out a cobra-like jab and caught the kid squarely on the chin. *Whack.* Another lightning jab, another bull's-eye. *Whack. Whack.*

It was over in ten seconds. The humiliated bully admitted defeat by turning and running, probably straight to the arms of mommy.

We gathered around Peter and slapped him on the back. None of us had imagined in our wildest dreams that he had some Joe Frazier in him. As excited as we were, his stoic demeanor never changed. He explained that his father had taught him some rudimentary boxing lessons for this very occasion. Word of Peter's fists of fury spread quickly, and no one ever messed with him again.

But I wouldn't go so far as to call him an athlete, at least not by the standard definition. I don't recall him ever joining us in our sandlot baseball, kickball, or football games. He was always at home building some sort of contraption in his garage or doing a chemistry experiment in his basement.

He did, however, excel at a street game we invented. A bunch of us would gather in the evenings on Whittaker Avenue, in front of his house, and pick teams of four or five. The respective teams lined up about thirty yards from each other and took turns throwing a Frisbee. The object was to score a goal by throwing it so that no defender could catch it before it landed past a designated crack in the street. We experimented with all kinds of shots – the skip off the cement, the frozen rope at the weakest defender, the floater that would get caught up in the wind and do unpredictable things.

Peter came up with his own shot – undoubtedly after studying the aerodynamics of the Frisbee in a wind tunnel – and named it the Whip-Wham-Whistling-Winger. He threw the Frisbee high in the air on a steep angle that made it curve sharply and descend at warp speed. Everyone had a hard time defending the Whip-Wham-Whistling-Winger. It was like trying to catch Sandy Koufax.

After seeing Peter's success with the shot, the rest of us tried it, but none of us could master the technique. The Frisbee usually just sailed harmlessly out of bounds. Like Rick Barry's underhand free-throw shooting and Arnold Palmer's pants hitch, the Whip-Wham-Whistling-Winger was Peter's calling card and his alone. I think he still holds the record for career goals scored on Whittaker Avenue.

Peter might not have been able to catch a baseball or throw a spiral, but he could do just about anything else. He taught himself how to play classical music on the piano. He designed model rockets (see "Frisky the Gerbil-naut"), bagged the components in plastic, illustrated the packaging, and actually got the hobby shop in Cudahy to sell a few. He was a talented artist, writing and illustrating his own comic books and painting watercolor landscapes. He was a beekeeper with six or eight hives in his backyard. He ordered and built a harpsichord from a kit. He spent one summer converting a washing machine into a working submarine and planned to test it in Lake Michigan before his father scuttled the project, fearing Peter would sink to a watery grave.

He did all this while in grade school.

In the summer, when we bored of catching tadpoles and building forts in the A&P swamp, Peter and I and our third musketeer, John Kresl, would walk a few blocks to Kinnickinnic Avenue and catch the bus for downtown, where we would spend hours roaming the Milwaukee Public Museum. Peter knew more about the exhibits than just about anybody, including the curators. He was a walking encyclopedia.

He also was double-jointed in both thumbs, and when he explained things, his slender fingers moved in a manner I would describe as delicate. For effect, or perhaps absently, he popped his thumbs in and out of their sockets.

You couldn't take your eyes off them.

One day he told me the U.S. Army was working on biowarfare programs and would someday have in its arsenal a microbe that could eat through steel and take down a bridge in minutes. Mind you, we were ten or eleven years old. He somehow just knew stuff like that.

Peter got me hooked me on astronomy, chemistry, entomology, model rocketry, tropical fish, rock collecting, Tom Swift, and just about anything else that could possibly interest a boy growing up in middle-class America in the 1960s.

By the time we were seniors in high school, he'd grown into a strapping young man, 6 feet, 2 inches tall and broad-shouldered, a back-stroker on the swim team and the lead in school plays. He was a class officer, served on the student council and somehow found time to join AFS, the forensics team, German club, the yearbook staff, pep club and, of course, National Honor Society. Oh, and he also made a short, animated horror flick called *The Living Woods* (starring yours truly as a kid who gets eaten by trees) that made its world premiere in the school auditorium.

His photograph appears no fewer than nineteen times in our senior yearbook. One of the photos bears the caption "This is the American Dream." And somebody took a whiz in this kid's shoe?

Peter went off to Loyola University in Louisiana on, of all things, an ROTC scholarship. I attended the University of Wisconsin-Whitewater, and we drifted apart. My senior year, three buddies and I packed into a car and drove to New Orleans for spring break. I remembered Peter telling me he lived near an old, red-brick fire station, not far from campus. On a lark, I suggested we look for him, but considering we didn't have his phone number or address, the odds of finding him were remote.

We drove around near the Loyola campus until we found an old, red-brick fire station ... and there he was, walking down the block with an impressive load of books under his arm. Peter Markiewicz! We pulled over and he stopped dead in his tracks and gave me the same calm and detached look I'd seen a million times growing up. He directed us to his apartment and we hung out for a few days and talked about old times and our plans for the future. We made nightly forays into the French Quarter, after which we stumbled back to his roach-infested pad. Finally, it was time to say goodbye.

That was April 1978. It was the last time I saw him.

Peter did his doctoral research at the University of Chicago. In the 1980s, he worked on infectious disease vaccines at the United States Army Medical Research Institute of Infectious Diseases – hey, maybe he came up with a defense for the steel-eating bacteria! – and subsequently worked on protein evolution at UCLA.

In 1993 he left UCLA to cofound Indiespace, the first web-based arts and entertainment company. After 2001 Indiespace became a consultancy, and Peter began to specialize in the impact of new media on society. He coauthored a landmark book, *Millennials and Pop Culture*. In 2005 he was team leader for Team Robomonster, a robotic, self-driving rock crawler entered in the Defense Advanced Research Projects Agency Grand Challenge, a prize competition for autonomous vehicles.

In recent years Peter has developed seminars on the millennial generation, pop culture and virtual worlds for the University of Southern California's Communication Technology Management programs at the Marshall School of Business. He has also taught interactive and web design at the Art Institute of California.

Geesh, what an underachiever.

When I think about Peter and all the goofy things we did, I can't help but shake my head and smile. He showed me single-cell organisms through a microscope and Saturn's rings through a telescope. Thanks to him, I learned how to play Beethoven's "Für Elise" on the piano (albeit poorly) and which chemicals to mix to make disappearing ink. I'm certain I gained a few IQ points just by osmosis.

That all happened a lifetime ago, but sometimes it feels like yesterday. I couldn't have asked for a better, smarter, more loyal friend with whom to share some of the best years of my life. And still, to this day, I wonder … who *did* take a whiz in Markiewicz's shoe?

Chapter 5

FIFTH-GRADE THIEF

In the 1960s, show and tell in elementary school was nearly as popular as playing dodgeball during recess, and you were far less likely to get hurt. I don't know how it's done today – probably virtually with Microsoft Teams – but back then kids brought actual objects to school, stood in front of the class, and explained what made their particular object interesting.

Sometimes, the object wasn't very interesting at all: an uncle's postcard from Germany, a Wall Drug bumper sticker, an antique Coke bottle. Show and tell could be a snooze-fest, but occasionally some kid brought in his father's Purple Heart from the Korean War or a foul ball from a Braves game at County Stadium, and that made it easier to sit through the dissertation on the hunk of granite from summer vacation in Paducah, Kentucky.

One day, in fifth-grade show and tell at Willow Glen Elementary, a girl brought in a miniature copy of the *Milwaukee Journal*. It was an exact replica of the newspaper, but one-tenth the size. You could make out the photos and read the headlines, but you needed a magnifying class to read the stories.

It was the coolest thing I'd ever seen and perhaps foreshadowed my forty-year career as a newspaper sportswriter. After the kids explained their objects, they were placed on a table, and you could take them to your desk and examine them.

I took the tiny paper, but instead of returning it to the table when I finished looking it over, I opened my desk and stuck it between the pages of a textbook. I don't know why, but I wanted that little newspaper. I had never before stolen anything in my ten years on earth.

At the end of the school day, the girl realized her tiny newspaper was missing and started to cry. Our teacher, Mrs. Poehling, asked that whoever had forgotten to return the item should do so now. For a brief moment, I thought about retrieving the paper from my textbook, handing it to Mrs. Poehling, and apologizing for being forgetful. But when she repeated her request, this time more forcefully, fear gripped me. It was too late now.

I was officially a thief.

Mrs. Poehling asked us to open our desks and make triple sure that we didn't have the little paper, which now seemingly had the value of the Hope Diamond. Like all the other kids, I dutifully lifted my desk top and noisily rummaged around, my face growing redder by the minute. The second hand on the classroom clock slowed to a crawl. I felt eyes staring at the back of my head. Had someone seen me? Would I be ratted out?

Finally, we were dismissed. I grabbed the textbook and bolted from the room. The girl was still crying, and I looked over my shoulder to see Mrs. Poehling consoling her. Guilt washed over me, and suddenly I felt lower than Bob Uecker's batting average.

I ran all the way home in a panic, flung open the door, and immediately hid the miniature newspaper under the refrigerator. It was the fifth-grade equivalent of robbing a bank and burying the loot in a tin can.

Every day for the next few weeks, I surreptitiously checked to make sure the little newspaper was in its hiding spot. By now, I was sure the St. Francis police were on the case. I expected a knock at my door and imagined my parents watching in horror as I was placed in handcuffs and hauled away to jail. Eventually, I'd be sentenced to do hard time at a juvenile correction facility.

The fear gradually subsided, but the guilt stayed with me as a little stain on my soul. I never again knowingly stole anything, though as an obnoxious teen I once pretended to pocket a waitress's tip at Marc's Big Boy, for which I was reamed out by the manager. My buddies thought it was hilarious.

Eventually, mothers clean under the refrigerator, and I could only imagine my mom's surprise when a tiny *Milwaukee Journal* emerged with the dust bunnies and assorted food crumbs. When she asked about it, I fessed up and got a stern lecture.

If the girl whose newspaper was taken during show and tell at Willow Glen in 1965 is reading this, I'm truly sorry. And I promise, I'll never do it again.

Chapter 6

FEAR STRIKES OUT

Kids today have a thousand different sports and activities vying for their attention and participation in the summer months. Back in the mid-1960s, we didn't have sports camps, water parks, arcades, video games, or the Disney Channel. Parents didn't rent bounce houses or throw swimming pool parties; on really hot days, we ran through the sprinkler and ate homemade popsicles.

It was rumored that girls met in small, giggling groups and listened to 45s on their record players. Occasionally, we saw them playing hopscotch or jumping rope Double Dutch-style. But who among us boys really knew what went on in their world?

This is not a knock on soccer, the most popular sport in the world, but no one in my neighborhood played the game. For all I know, soccer wasn't invented until 1999, when Brandi Chastain ripped off her jersey after scoring the winning touchdown in the World Cup Bowl … or something like that.

In the 1960s, what we had was baseball. Our summers revolved around the game. Once, Frank Mahuta's parents took a bunch of us to a Milwaukee Braves game at County Stadium. We sat in the old sundeck along the first base line and screamed Hank Aaron's name every time The Hammer trotted out to his position in right field. In the third or fourth inning, he turned and waved to us. I can still see him, standing in the greenest grass in the world, in that beautiful Braves uniform. Chill bumps.

My collection of '60s baseball cards would be worth tens of thousands of dollars today, but my mother, of course, threw them out. This seems to be a universal truth. Even Bob Koehler, a kid on our block whose dad bought him packs by the thirty-six-count box – the rest of us could afford to buy them only one nickel pack at a time – told me years later that his mom tossed his entire collection, which today would make "Bobby the K" richer than Jeff Bezos and Warren Buffett combined. (Koehler, incidentally, has attended every Milwaukee Brewers home game since 1983.)

I sharpened my baseball fielding skills by throwing a rubber ball against the brick front of our house, until my mom, doing dishes, invariably yelled out the kitchen window that the repeated thud of the ball was driving her crazy. I practiced my hitting by tossing stones into the air and whacking them with a plastic Wiffle bat.

In 1966, at age ten, I joined the Cudahy-St. Francis Little League and after tryouts, was assigned to the minor-league Senators. The minors were for the kids who weren't, for lack of a kinder description, any good. We got T-shirts, while the major leaguers got full uniforms – heavy flannel jerseys and pants modeled after real baseball uniforms. They even got stirrup socks.

My best friend, John Kresl, went straight to the majors. Frank Mahuta, a year older than me, beat me to the major leagues, too. I was envious and determined to join them … someday.

The problem was that I was deathly afraid of facing live pitching. And in the field, I prayed that the batter would hit the ball anywhere but toward me. Despite all the pitches I threw against our house and all the stones I smashed with my Wiffle bat, I had zero confidence. I was right where I should have been. I was a minor-leaguer. I wasn't any good.

When the games started, I stood in the batter's box with the bat on my shoulder and took every pitch. I was either going to strike out looking or walk. My parents, sitting in the bleachers, shouted words of encouragement when I headed back to the dugout after yet another strikeout and praised my "good eye" when I walked.

I don't know what made me finally swing at a pitch. Maybe I got tired of the opposing team's chatter – *We got a looker here* – or perhaps the embarrassment of striking out so often finally turned to anger. Whatever it was, something inside me screamed "NOW!" I swung the bat with all my might and watched in amazement as the ball rose majestically into the blue sky, perhaps thirty feet or so at its highest point, and plopped down in foul territory behind first base.

A chill went up and down my spine. Even the opposing team's parents cheered.

Though I wound up striking out yet again, this time it was swinging and not looking. It went down as a K in the scorebook, but it felt like a grand slam. As corny as it sounds, that foul ball I hit as a ten-year-old Little Leaguer remains one of the defining moments of my life. I had broken free from the paralyzing fear that held me vise-like in its grip. I'd put a dent in my feelings of inadequacy. It's instructive that I don't recall my first base hit, or the ones that followed, but I remember that foul ball in vivid detail, as if it happened yesterday.

I wouldn't say I instantly transformed into Willie Mays or Mickey Mantle, but from that point on, I swung the bat, occasionally with good results.

The next year, my father volunteered to coach a minor-league team and made sure I was on his roster. In our season opener at Greene Park, I was the winning pitcher and cracked a home run. I still remember the score: 20-5. I don't know if I've done anything in my life that has made me prouder than playing for my dad and helping him win his first game.

The night after that game, I was in bed when he came home from a Little League meeting and woke me up. The major-league Tigers wanted me. I'd been waiting for this moment, but now I didn't want to go. I wanted to play for my dad.

"Gary, you're too good for the minors," he said. "I want you on my team, but you're ready for this."

The next week, I made my debut for the Tigers in right field and collected my first hit, off Frank Mahuta, no less. We went on to win the American League title and played in the 1967 Cudahy-St. Francis Little League World Series.

That was all good. But nothing would ever replace the feeling I had when I swung at a pitch for the first time and watched the ball soar into the sky, opening a world in which anything was possible.

Chapter 7

FRISKY THE GERBIL-NAUT

The crude video game *Pong* was still the stuff of science fiction in the 1960s, and hard as it is to believe, not a single kid in the whole wide world owned a cellphone, an iPad, or a smartwatch. (Note: some kids today cannot read a clock.)

Instead, we had hobbies. I'm pretty sure it was some kind of law in the '60s that every kid had to collect or build something.

We lived one mile from the Cudahy Hobby Shop, where we usually spent the entirety of our allowances, our hard-earned paper route money, and occasionally the change from the bottom of our mothers' purses (I confess only because the statute of limitations has expired). The "B-Hob Shop," as we so cleverly called it (reversing the syllables in "hobby), also peddled my drug of choice: Hot Dog bubble gum. I quickly became an addict and walked around with perpetually red teeth.

Some kids collected stamps, others collected coins, and still others put together model cars. Me? For two years, I spent every penny I had on tropical fish. I had so many fish tanks that I could have charged admission to my bedroom. My grandfather, who emigrated from Sicily and spoke broken English, once stayed with us for a week after a small fire broke out at his house. My Mom asked him one morning, "Pa, how are you sleeping?" He said, "Okay, okay. But what that noise, 'blub, blub, blub?'"

It was the air filters in my aquariums. I had five tanks set up, including a saltwater tank, which was home to a sea urchin and a pair of clownfish; a twenty-gallon tank that showcased, among other things, a school of brightly colored Neon tetras, a pair of aggressive Angelfish, and a blind cave fish with a voracious appetite; a ten-gallon breeding tank for my swordfish; and a five-gallon tank that held my two prized piranhas.

Once, our neighbor from two doors down, an Army recruiter named Charlie Glady, was over visiting my parents and obviously had had one too many beers. I told him about my piranhas, with their little, razor-sharp teeth and their lust for blood. I'd read that in their native habitat, the Amazon River inSouth America, schools of carnivorous piranhas were known to devour large animals that wandered into the water, stripping away the flesh in seconds. Unimpressed, Mr. Glady dismissed me with a wave of the hand. Slurring his words, he demanded a razor blade, and when my father produced one, he walked over to the piranha tank, cut his finger and thrust his hand into the water, staring at me in defiance. Not two seconds later, he shrieked like a little girl and jumped three feet into the air. One of the little critters had bitten him.

When I grew out of my tropical fish phase, I looked around for a new hobby, and that's when I discovered model rocketry. Model rockets were constructed from plastic, cardboard tubing and balsa wood and came in ready-to-build kids from Estes Industries in Colorado. You cut the fins from a thin sheet of balsa, glued them to the body tube, attached the nose cone, and spray-painted the finished rocket. Then you launched it with a single-use engine that cost anywhere from forty cents to two dollars depending on the size and amount of propellant. The engine was supposed to be ignited with a battery-powered launcher, but more often than not, we simply stuck a length of fuse in the thing, lit it with a match and scurried for cover as the rocket shot off the pad with a signature "pffffwwwwt."

At first, we built and launched rudimentary rockets that flew only a few hundred feet into the air and tumbled back to the ground, occasionally in one piece. But as we became more skilled at rocket building, we advanced to sleek, multistage beauties that reached heights of 2,500 feet and returned safely to earth after a small ejection charge in the engine deployed a parachute. On a windy day, your rocket could wind up a half-mile from its launch pad, descending gracefully into the backyard of an unsuspecting woman hanging laundry to dry. That was always good for a laugh.

One day, Peter Markiewicz came over with a small, round, black-and-white photograph.

"What's that?" I asked, peering at the tiny image.

"Your garage," he said.

Sure enough, it was an aerial photo taken with Camroc, the pride of the Estes fleet. The rocket was fairly sophisticated for the 1960s, when Slinky and Silly Putty were all the rage and color television was still a novelty. The camera shuttle was triggered just after Camroc reached its apogee and the parachute deployed. We launched it dozens of times that summer and took aerial photos of half of St. Francis, but eventually even that got old.

We were ready for the next step. We were ready to launch a live payload.

Some of the more expensive rockets had clear plastic payload tubes in which you could send ants, grasshoppers, or earthworms on the ride of their lives. Considering that an earthworm doesn't have much of a vertical leap, flying a couple thousand feet into the air had to be a rush. We customized one payload tube by waterproofing it, and on a cold winter's day, we launched a small catfish into the stratosphere. The thing lived through the ordeal and I returned it to the aquarium, where it spent the remainder of its life happily scavenging for tropical fish poop.

As spring approached, Mr. Holson, our sixth-grade teacher at Willow Glen Elementary School, suggested we come up with a class science project. Peter volunteered to build the mother of all rocket ships, and I reluctantly agreed to let my pet gerbil, Frisky, become a pioneering gerbil-naut. Peter would design and build the rocket, I would serve as his first mate and go-fer, and the rest of the kids in class would study rockets and write reports. Frisky would continue to eat and poop until the big day.

Over the next few weeks, the behemoth took shape in Peter's basement. Since there was no rocket big enough to carry a gerbil as payload, Peter literally built the thing from scratch. Eight engines, firing simultaneously, would carry the four-foot-tall rocket – and Frisky – high enough to register on the radar at nearby Billy Mitchell Field (now Mitchell International Airport). An oversized, custom-made parachute would deliver the precious payload safely back to earth.

Frisky, who would pull ten Gs, probably would be scared enough to empty his teeny-tiny gerbil bowels, but would otherwise be unscathed.

Finally, launch day arrived and Mr. Holson led the class outdoors, where Peter had the rocket set up on its launch pad on the football field. It was a magnificent-looking thing, painted black and white and gleaming in the sun. The class gathered around as I dutifully placed Frisky on a shock-absorbing bed of grass in the payload tube. He looked back at us, wiggling his nose in that cute gerbil way, as if to say, "When's lunch served?"

All the girls sighed and one of them squealed, "Ooh, he's so cute!" I made a mental note about girls liking gerbils.

We gathered in a circle, a safe distance from the rocket, and Peter began the countdown. The class counted backward from ten in unison and yelled, "Blast-off!" Peter ignited the engines, and for a pregnant second, the rocket shook on the launch pad, smoke billowing out in all directions. Then slowly, majestically, it lifted off the pad and quickly gained speed as it roared toward the heavens.

Oh, what a sight! I could imagine Frisky saying, *"Wh-a-a-t?"* and trying to process the experience in his little gerbil brain. For a few seconds, he would be nearly crushed by his own body weight, but then the terrifying sensation would go away and he would float peacefully back to earth, looking down at us and still wondering about lunch.

As the engines burned the last of the propellant, the rocket reached its apogee and started to arc over for its return trip to earth, so high in the sky that it appeared to be a mere speck. Peter announced, "The parachute should deploy in five seconds."

The class counted down again: "Five ... four ... three ... two ... one!" The parachute did not deploy.

Genuinely puzzled but seemingly unconcerned, Peter calmly said, "The parachute should be deploying. Why is it not deploying?"

We watched in horror as the rocket headed nose first back to earth, like a dart thrown from the heavens. There was not going to be a happy ending.

Frisky was not going to emerge, wiggle his nose, and ask for lunch. The poor little guy was seconds away from giving his life for science.

The girls started screaming, and several of them were already in tears when the rocket thudded heavily into the ground at the far end of the football field and caught fire. Joe Euringer, who brought his father's eight-millimeter camera to record the event for posterity, was first to reach the crash site.

"Save Frisky!" I yelled as I sprinted toward the smoke. "Pull him out!"

Joe kept filming, oblivious to my cries. Frisky was on his way to gerbil heaven, where lunch is always served.

As I turned away from the crash, sick to my stomach, another amazing scene was unfolding. The girls, every last one of them, had formed a posse and were chasing Peter across the football field screaming, "Murderer! You killed Frisky!" Peter was running for his life with his peculiar, stiff-legged gait. He reached the ten-foot-tall cyclone fence at the end of the field and was scaling it, halfway to freedom, when the girls grabbed him by the ankles, dragged him down, and began pummeling him. I ran over to the melee, not so much to defend Peter as to watch girls throw punches.

Ever the pacifist, Peter was shielding his face with his arms and trying to explain himself, but the girls were having none of his scientific mumbo jumbo. They bloodied his nose and threatened him with further bodily harm until Mr. Holson finally got everybody calmed down. We filed solemnly back into the classroom.

Actually, other than the mob violence, it was a good teaching moment. We learned a lot about rocket science, though we never did figure out why the parachute failed to deploy, and Peter's "Ode to Estes" became "Frisky's Flying Coffin." Peter surmised that the fireproof recovery wadding, which prevents the ejection charge from melting the parachute, had gotten stuck in the airframe and acted as a stopper, something like the cork in a bottle of wine. We also learned a little about human nature and vigilante justice. Dirty Harry had nothing on the girls in Mr. Holson's sixth-grade class.

We wrote our science papers and, eventually, the happy life and tragic death of Frisky the Gerbil-naut was forgotten. Just before school let out for the summer, however, Joe Euringer brought his eight-millimeter film to school, and for reasons beyond all comprehension, Mr. Holson allowed him to show it to our class.

In the darkened room, we once again watched the rocket take flight and off camera heard Peter saying, "The parachute should deploy in five seconds." Then came the final countdown, the fatal crash, and the camera jiggling as Joe ran to the site. Finally, there was the horrific close-up of poor little Frisky, in his death throes.

I heard a few sniffles and a couple of sobs. The girls were becoming emotional all over again.

Alarms went off in my head. I looked around for Peter, but he was gone. Above the crying, I heard the slap of his shoes as he ran down the hall to the safety of the principal's office.

The D'Amato family, circa 1968. From left, front row: Gary, Nancy, David, and Linda
Back: Peter.

Bolivar Avenue in St. Francis in 1968. All the houses look the same.

The 1967 Cudahy-St. Francis American League champion Tigers. Gary is in the front row, second from the left. One of his best friends, Clark Chiaverotti, is in the front row, far right. Clark's brother, Curtis, is sitting to Gary's left. Nearly fifty years later, Gary would play with Curtis in a men's senior baseball league.

Gary's first Little League team, the Senators. He's in the front row, second from left. His close friend, Frank Mahuta, is in the front row, fourth from the left.

Gary, Linda, and David, ages 10, 9, and 6, in 1966.

Linda and Gary assume the television-watching position in front of the set with a rabbit-ear antenna.

Gary's sixth-grade class at Willow Glen Elementary School that bore witness to Frisky the Gerbil-naut's demise. Peter Markiewicz, who built Frisky's flying coffin, is second from left in the third row. Joe Euringer, who filmed Frisky's death for posterity, is on the far left, second row. Henry Brazil, one of Gary's best friends, is second from right, third row. John Kresl, another bestie, is far right, second row. Gary is far left, fourth row.

· OCT · 62

Gary's dad, Peter, center, the deer hunter who never shot a deer, is flanked by two hunting buddies.

Gary's friend, Peter Markiewicz, taken during a third-grade field trip to the Milwaukee Public Museum.

Chapter 8

THE A&P SWAMP

It wasn't the Everglades or the Okefenokee Swamp, but on the southwest side of St. Francis we had our own little marshy wonder, where we could catch tadpoles, build forts and, of course, get soakers.

Just a couple hundred yards from busy Layton Avenue, behind a row of identical brick ranches on Cudahy Avenue and next to a strip mall, the A&P Swamp was two or three acres of shallow marsh, cattails, and willow groves – a tiny oasis of nature hidden in plain sight, smack dab in the middle of concrete and commerce.

Kids today probably have a swamp app on their smartphones, but we had the real thing.

It came about its name honestly, being that it was a couple hundred yards from the Atlantic & Pacific grocery store that anchored the strip mall. In the 1960s, A&P stores were as big as Publix and Kroger are today. Alas, the store is long gone, as is the swamp. That's progress, I guess.

The A&P Swamp was the popular place to hang out for kids who attended Willow Glen Elementary School, just a few blocks to the north. We'd ride our bikes to the swamp, but our first stop always was the Rexall Drugstore next to the A&P, where we'd peruse the comic books and blow our allowance on Sweetarts, Razzles, Laffy Taffy, Bazooka bubble gum, jawbreakers, and whatever else would give us a mouthful of cavities.

High on sugar, we'd head over to the swamp. This was a time when you could set your bike on its kickstand or lay it down in the grass, disappear for two or three hours, and come back to find the bike exactly where you left it.

Bicycle rustling was not yet a common criminal activity.

Once in the swamp, there were a million things to do. In the late spring and early summer, you could catch tadpoles by the dozen with little nets, keep them in glass jars with holes punched in the metal lids and watch them grow legs and turn into frogs. You could catch butterflies flitting around the wildflowers and honeybees pollinating the purple clover. You could pick cattails, dry them out in the sun, and light them at dusk (the pungent smoke from the "punks" was said to keep away mosquitoes).

Old boards and planks placed one after another in the shallow water allowed you to walk out into the middle of the swamp. This exercise tested your balance and coordination; one false move and you wound up with a soaker (i.e., a waterlogged sneaker). Occasionally, someone would fall in and emerge covered in smelly muck. Our mothers must have loved doing our laundry.

Once, jumping from board to board, I landed on a protruding, rusty nail, which penetrated my tennis shoe and skewered my foot. A trip to the doctor for a tetanus shot made for a lesson well learned. From that point on, I watched where I jumped. Experience, they say, is the best teacher.

Teenagers sometimes came to the swamp, claimed it as their own, and obnoxiously dumped out our jars of pollywogs, which we'd worked painstakingly to catch. We'd retreat to our forts in the willow groves and plot their extermination.

At the end of the day, if we had a few pennies left, we went back to the drugstore to replenish our dwindling supply of sweets for the ride home, where supper inevitably was waiting on the table. Our parents didn't have to ask where we were; our soggy shoes and dirty T-shirts were dead giveaways.

I don't know if the world would be a better place if city kids today had access to a swamp and were left to their own devices without parents hovering nearby to monitor sugar intake, lather on SPF 50 sunscreen every thirty minutes and warn about rusty nails.

But I do know this: you could watch the Nature channel all day long and not learn half the things we learned in the A&P Swamp.

Chapter 9

HEAVY METAL THUNDER

At about twelve years old, I started to change the way boys at that age change. Call it puberty or call it an awakening, but I began to notice shapely and seductive things that turned my head and made my heart pound. Desire gave way to lust, which gave way to single-minded obsession.

I had to have one. I had to feel one throbbing beneath me, pulsating between my legs, thrilling me in ways pubescent boys should not be thrilled.

I just had to have … a motorcycle.

"A *motorcycle*?" my mother asked, using the same tone she reserved for,

"You did *what* to your sister?"

I was just a few seconds into my sales pitch, and already the door had been slammed in my face, the Doberman was growling in the window, and the cops were on their way. It would now be extremely difficult to complete the transaction.

"A motorcycle?" she repeated. "Why on earth would you want a motorcycle?"

Sometimes, moms ask stupid questions.

Why on earth? To feel older and cooler, to feel the wind in my face, to feel the rumble of the engine, to impress my friends, to be daring and dangerous and free, to be just like Michael Parks in the ultra-hip television series, *Then Came Bronson.*

"You will never have a motorcycle," she said with chilling finality.

I immediately turned to Plan B.

"Dad?"

I struck the pose, appropriately tentative and humble. If I would have been wearing a hat, it would have been in hand. My father was hiding behind the newspaper. Was it a silent sign of sympathy, or did he just want to stay out of an argument he could not possibly win?

"Pete, you tell him right now that he cannot have a motorcycle!" "Hmmmpf," Dad said.

I was encouraged. He did not say no.

The days went by that summer, and so did the motorcycles. I noticed every one of them, the Triumphs and Hondas and Suzukis and Yamahas. I learned to tell the distinctive rumbling *potato-potato* of the Harley-Davidson from the tinny whine of the two-strokers. I bought biker magazines and devoured articles on motocross racing and tricked-out choppers. Well okay, it's possible that I also noticed the pictures of the babes, wearing bikinis and draped suggestively over the custom-painted gas tanks of outrageous hogs.

I rode my green Schwinn five-speed bicycle around the block over and over, twisting the right handlebar grip as if it were the throttle, alternately humming the theme music from *Then Came Bronson* and making "vroom" noises.

Yeah, right.

Then came Bronson. There goes D'Amato, the kid with a crush on motorcycles. What a sap.

One day, I walked into the house and my father was sitting at the kitchen table waiting for me. He pointed to a set of keys and said, "Go look in the garage." My mom started saying something about "this is a very bad idea, Pete," but I was gone, setting a world record for the sixty-foot sprint (Side Door to Garage Door Division).

I flung open the door and there it was: a gorgeous, red-and-cream Honda … scooter. Ninety cubic centimeters of heavy metal thunder, a two-speed with no clutch, floorboards instead of pedals, gas tank under the seat.

Man, it was impressive.

Standing orders from the old man were that I could ride the Honda up and down the alley behind our house, and that was it. I was far too young to legally drive a car, let alone apply for a motorcycle permit. Plus, we lived about four hundred yards from the St. Francis Police Station. I guess my dad figured that if the cops saw me riding in the alley, they'd probably tell me to park it and let me off with a stern lecture. I wasn't going to go to jail for terrorizing the neighborhood on a ninety cc, step-through Honda scooter.

But that wild stallion was meant to be tamed. Confining me to the alley on that Honda was like giving a kid a BB gun and telling him he couldn't shoot tin cans off his younger brother's head. So, a few days later, while Dad and Mom were at work, I held my breath and walked the scooter right past the cop shop and down Nicholson Avenue to my friend Bruce's house, which had a long gravel driveway and a big yard. Better yet, his parents weren't home.

Perfect for pushing the envelope.

We took turns doing slow circles in the grass for a while, and then I got the brilliant idea that invariably occurs to a twelve-year-old kid riding anything with two wheels and a combustible engine. "I'm going to see how fast I can get it to go," I said. The idea was to start at the back of the gravel driveway, which was more than two hundred feet long, and brake before I got to Nicholson Avenue.

The plan worked to perfection.

Until I got to the braking part.

Hurtling like a rocket toward the unknown, I approached the end of the driveway doing maybe twenty-five miles per hour. Then I went blank. Now what? At the last second, before roaring onto Nicholson Avenue and quite possibly T-boning a car, I locked up the rear brake but forgot to release the throttle. I very adroitly compounded the error by turning the wheel sharply to the right while still moving at a pretty good clip.

It was a spectacular crash, gravel and chunks of sod flying everywhere, me and the bike cartwheeling across the lawn. After completing three somersaults with a half-twist, I sat up, stunned and scared out of my mind. I quickly checked to make sure all my limbs were still attached. I was alive!

Then, like the scene in a war movie in which the soldier slowly regains his hearing after a bomb explodes nearby, I became conscious of the Honda, on its side, the throttle stuck wide open. The poor little engine was screaming bloody murder, and smoke was billowing from the manifold. I crawled over on all fours and turned off the ignition. Bruce came running.

"Whadja do that for?" he asked, his eyes bulging out of their sockets.

"That was some wild ride," I managed, trying to sound cool as I picked tiny pieces of gravel out of my left forearm. "You want to try it?"

Bruce turned and ran into his house, slamming the door behind him.

Gingerly, I got up, dusted myself off and picked up the bike. Other than a couple of loose spokes and scratches, it was none the worse for wear. I limped it home, parked it in the garage, and swore off riding for at least twenty-four hours.

But a funny thing happened at Willow Glen Elementary School early that fall. I somehow made the transformation from geeky bookworm to almost most popular kid. The Honda had given me status among my classmates. Even Rick Moody, an edgy kid who wore black T-shirts and never joined our pickup base-ball or football games, had taken a semi-liking to me. Rick was a year older than I, somehow had access to a motorcycle – a real one, not a scooter – and smoked cigarettes. He walked around the playground shouting, "I am the em-peror!" and no one ever called him on it. He was considered by many to be an honest-to-goodness hood (short for hoodlum).

"Let's go riding Saturday," Rick said, "on the tracks."

He was eyeing me and grinning. Did I have guts or was I a wimpy alley rider?

"Sure," I said with a no-big-deal shoulder shrug. "On the tracks."

The railroad tracks ran through the west side of St. Francis, and a dirt path, perhaps eighteen inches wide, extended farther south along the tracks than I had ever walked. No one knew where the path ended. Chicago? New Orleans? Guatemala? The tracks ran under a series of dilapidated wooden bridges and along the east side of General Mitchell Field. Once you got south of the airport, there were few houses and endless fields.

I needed backup on this one. Henry Brazil lived down the block from Rick and agreed to be my riding mate. By that time, Frank Mahuta's father had bought him a one hundred twenty-five cc Suzuki, a beautiful black and chrome machine. We practically had our own biker gang.

On a sunny Saturday morning, I walked my bike down the alley and met Henry. I told my parents we were going to ride in his big backyard, but instead we crossed Pennsylvania Avenue and fired up the Honda. Rick and Frank were waiting for us in a field near the tracks. I was filled with a sense of foreboding, but it was too late to turn back. After we took turns jumping the bikes off a little dirt hill – I might have caught twelve inches of air – we started down the nar-row, rutted path in single file. Rick led the pack, Frank was second, and I was third, with Henry holding on for dear life on the back and giggling in my ear.

We rode for some twenty minutes, and then the path turned precarious. The gentle hill on the left became a steep drop-off. It was ten feet straight down from the track bed to a tangle of underbrush and swamp. There was no margin for error. One miscalculated turn of the wheel, and we were going to be swimming with the pollywogs. To my relief, Rick put up his hand and we stopped, stood the bikes on their kickstands and took a break. We were tossing stones into the water and Rick was on his second cigarette when Frank glanced to his right, bolted to his feet and yelled, "Train!"

In the distance, but growing bigger by the second, a fast-moving freight train was barreling toward us.

We scrambled up the embankment and jumped on our bikes, and two of them roared to life. The third – mine, of course – wouldn't start. We had agreed that Henry would drive home, so he was trying to kick-start the Honda, I was yelling in his ear, and the train was closing in on us, its whistle blasting.

Finally, like a scene out of the movies, the engine sputtered and caught, and Henry twisted the throttle, kicking gravel behind us. We fishtailed out of there, me in back, stealing glances over my shoulder at the train. It was gaining on us.

"Faster!" I shouted above the engine's whine. "Come on!"

It must have been quite a sight: two stupid kids on a Honda scooter, alternately screaming and gritting their teeth as the little bike bounced and bucked on the rutted path, a bellowing freight train on their tail.

Rick and Frank were hundreds of yards ahead of us, two dots growing smaller in the distance. The Honda was giving us all she had. And the train was gaining, blasting its whistle every few seconds, the conductor undoubtedly dumbfounded by the scene unfolding in front of him.

We were goners. I could see the headline the next week in the *Cudahy-St. Francis Reminder-Enterprise:* "Two Members of Willow Glen Bike Gang Decapitated by Freight Train."

The thing seemed to be ten feet behind us now, billowing smoke and making the kind of noise you would not want to hear twice. I was self-administering the last rites when suddenly the path veered away from the tracks and into a field. As Henry steered to safety, the freight train roared past.

We had cheated death!

But we were not out of the woods. Henry's expert motocross driving had saved us, but in his excitement, he tried to steer out of a mud-caked rut and in an instant, we were airborne. Henry flew over the handlebars, and I flew over him, and the bike bounced drunkenly for fifteen or twenty feet before tumbling into a weed patch. We landed in a heap, practically on top of each other, and Henry started to giggle. Relief turned to anger. I could have punched him, but when he laughed, he made a raspy, high-pitched, cartoonish sound, and it was infectious. I started to giggle with him, and we lay in the grass, laughing our saddle-sore asses off. Thank God nothing was broken.

Frank and Rick doubled back and stopped near us, revving their throttles.

"We thought you guys were toast!" Frank said, and Rick the Emperor grinned and nodded. I got the distinct impression that if we had indeed perished, he would have fired up a celebratory cigarette and flicked a few ashes on our still-warm corpses before roaring away. He was one tough hood.

Bruised and battered, Henry and I walked the little Honda through the field, across Pennsylvania Avenue and down the alley. Before we parted, I said, "I don't think I'll be riding for a while, Henry." He studied me for several long seconds and nodded knowingly.

It was to be my final great adventure on the Honda. My motorcycle phase was coming to an end. The bike mostly sat in the garage that fall, and I finally got Dad's permission to sell it, loose spokes and all, to the Labisch brothers. My mother was never happier than the day Ronny and Bobby forked over a couple hundred dollars and drove away on "that thing."

Many years later, as an adult pushing forty, I would buy another motorcycle, a much bigger Honda, in what I suppose was an attempt to recapture the thrill I felt when I saddled up that little red-and-cream scooter.

Of course, it wasn't the same. How could it be? You only get one shot at being twelve years old.

Chapter 10

SPIN THE BOTTLE

On my thirteenth birthday, Henry Brazil invited me over to his house, ostensibly to work on our plan for putting together a garage band.

We'd been practicing Roy Orbison's "Oh, Pretty Woman" for a couple of weeks – me squeaking out the notes on alto saxophone, Henry semi-competently keeping the beat on an old snare drum – and now all we needed was to find another Lennon and McCartney in St. Francis and we'd be ready to rock ''n' roll.

Actually, I later did join a band, and we played "Georgy Girl" by The Seekers and "Windy" by The Association for an eighth-grade dance at Willow Glen. No girls threw panties at the stage. Or even paid attention to us.

But I digress.

We headed for the darkened basement, and when I got to the bottom step, Henry turned on the light and twenty classmates yelled "Surprise!" I should have guessed something was up when my mom bought me black-and-white checkered pants and an orange turtleneck at Sears & Roebuck for "band practice."

We mingled, the boys mostly on one half of the room, talking loudly and punching each other in the shoulder, the girls giggling and whispering and no doubt talking about which of us guys they'd go steady with. I'm pretty sure my name didn't come up.

At some point, Henry produced a record player, put on some 45s, and people started dancing. Having never danced, not even alone in my bedroom, I was mortified. But it soon became apparent that most of the boys had two or possibly three left feet, and after a few songs by Tommy James and the Shondells and Three Dog Night, I somehow found the courage to join the ritual and began jerking around spasmodically like everyone else.

Then things got a little weird. Henry turned off the lights, save for a red lava lamp, and produced an empty bottle.

It was time to play Spin the Bottle. The object of the game was not to hit a home run or score a goal, at least not in the traditional sense. The object was to kiss a member of the opposite sex.

We sat in a circle, alternating boy-girl. A boy spun the bottle until it pointed to a girl, or vice versa, and then the two had to kiss. For the love of God, could there possibly be a more awkward social activity? I don't know if teens play spin the bottle today, but it should be outlawed in all fifty states.

It's just like Russian roulette … and only slightly less dangerous.

You could tell by body language and bravado which of us were confident, at least outwardly, and which of us wished we were instead playing Stratego or

Monopoly, or even Twister, the last requiring some incidental physical contact, but no intentional lip-locking.

I held my breath as the bottle spun 'round and 'round. After six or seven spins, I was still a kissing virgin. Maybe I'd get lucky and escape with my fragile self-esteem intact.

Then it was Sue Medlin's turn. Sue was one of the more attractive girls in the eighth grade at Willow Glen, shy and willowy with long brown hair. She gave the bottle a healthy spin, and when it slowed to a stop, I was looking straight down the barrel of that snub-nose revolver posing as an empty Coke bottle.

I distinctly remember "Hey Jude" playing softly in the background. *"Hey Jude, don't be afraid; you were made to go out and get her."* Groovy. The Beatles were serenading us. I leaned in and semi-closed my eyes, not wanting to miss the target.

"Ewww," Sue said, turning up her pretty little nose.

I can say with some authority that it stings being emasculated at thirteen. Why is it that I can't remember what I had for lunch yesterday, but I can recall every detail about that moment, from the darkened room and the smell of the incense burning to the muffled giggles, right down to my black-and-white checked pants and orange turtleneck and the way my stomach churned?

I'm sure Sue meant no harm. It was just a natural reaction when the bottle pointed to a kid with thick glasses and early onset acne. I didn't say a word, but perhaps she could see the humiliation written on my face by the glow of the lava lamp. We both wanted to get it over with in the worst way. "OK," she said. Then we puckered up and touched lips for about six-tenths of a second.

Thankfully, neither one of us died or even got mono.

I have no idea what became of Sue Medlin or for that matter, most of the kids at the party that night. Henry and I drifted apart, as eighth-grade best friends often do. I went on to have a lot more birthdays, another fifty and counting. None, however, was as remarkable as that one.

Who forgets an awkward first kiss with a pretty girl, in a darkened basement, with "Hey Jude" playing in the background?

Chapter 11

HOW I CRACKED THEM UP

The worst thing about dying of embarrassment is that in most cases, unfortunately, you continue to live. As much as you wish you were dead or better yet, that all the people pointing at you and laughing were dead, what happens is that everybody continues to breathe, except for the ones who are laughing so hard they need oxygen.

Now, if you're thirteen years old and you suffer from a profound lack of self-confidence, and you are hopelessly and painfully tongue-tied around members of the opposite sex, and something unspeakable happens to you in your coed physical education class … well, that's a psychological scar that never heals. You could go on to win the Nobel Prize and the Heisman Trophy, invent time travel, marry a Swedish bikini model, and become president of the United States. But all it takes is for some wise guy at a class reunion to say, "Hey, remember that time in gym class when …" and you feel like the biggest dufus on the planet.

Though my encounter with the Grin Reaper occurred in 1969, it was so traumatic that it remains the subject of a recurring nightmare. My M.E.M. (Most Embarrassing Moment) became urban legend, at least in St. Francis, Wisconsin, and for all I know, my long-ago classmates are telling their grandchildren the story at this moment, and everybody is laughing so hard they're crying. It's the gift that keeps on giving.

So, go ahead. Yuk it up at my expense.

In the eighth grade at Willow Glen Elementary School, the boys and girls shared the gymnasium during physical education class. Usually, the teacher kept the boys on one half of the gym and the girls on the other. The boys would engage in healthful and productive activities such as murder-the-guy-with-the-ball in futile attempts to impress the girls, who couldn't have cared less about our pubescent preening. Occasionally, the sexes would intermingle for forty-five minutes of torture (i.e., ballroom dancing).

One day, as we changed from our school clothes into our T-shirts and shorts, Clark Chiaverotti and I were engrossed in conversation and suddenly realized we were the last boys in the locker room and class had started. Clark ran into the gym and I hurriedly followed.

Though the bell had rung, no formal activity had begun, and the boys and girls were still milling around. I casually strolled over to the water fountain and took a good, long drink.

My head was still in the porcelain when I felt a tap on my shoulder and glanced backward. It was Lloyd Everard, but I wasn't ready to give up the water fountain. He'd have to wait his turn.

"Gary," Lloyd said in a stage whisper, "you forgot to put your gym shorts on."

A chill swept over me, and it wasn't from the breeze I suddenly felt on my butt. I whirled around as laughter filled the gym. The girls were covering their mouths with their hands and giggling; the boys were not nearly as demure, pointing and slapping their knees, howling and punching one another on the shoulder. They had hit the comedy mother lode.

It was then, and remains to this day, the most horrific moment of my life.

I was standing there, facing the entire eighth-grade class, in a T-shirt, tennis shoes, socks … and my jockstrap. Good God almighty!

I sprinted to the locker room, the laughter echoing in my ears. I wanted to disappear from the face of the earth. I wanted to pack my bags right then and there, and move to the jungles of Bolivia. I was prepared to sit in the locker room for the rest of the period, for the rest of the day, for the rest of the school year. There was no way I was going back into that gym to face my tormentors.

Five minutes passed and Mr. Caldwell, the gym teacher, walked into the locker room with a look of fatherly concern on his face. I quickly wiped the tears from my cheeks as he came over and draped his arm around my shoulder. He assured me that only a few people had seen me butt-naked and that it was no big deal. He patiently explained that everybody would have a good laugh at my expense and then would forget about it pretty quickly. Within a week, he said, it would be old news, and some other monumental development would dominate the eighth-grade gossip mill.

To his credit, Mr. Caldwell was sympathetic to my plight and hastily decided that the class would see a movie that day. Everyone would sit quietly on the floor in the darkened gym and watch a snooze-inducing documentary about personal hygiene (which, thankfully, didn't include orifices). Mr. Caldwell, bless his soul, was trying to prevent me from suffering further psychological damage. I learned later that he addressed the class while I was in the locker room and said he didn't want to hear a peep when I emerged.

Eventually, he talked me down off the ledge. He told me to take my time and return to the gym only when I was ready. After a few more minutes, I tiptoed back in and rejoined my classmates, who were sitting on the floor and at least pretending to watch the movie. Even in the dark, I could feel every pair of eyes follow me. I heard a snicker or two and the pssp-pssp of a few kids whispering, but that was it. Back in the day, kids obeyed their teachers.

When school let out, I was the first one out the door and sprinted all the way home. I flung myself on my bed and got sick to my stomach thinking about all the ridicule I would face in the weeks ahead. I was too embarrassed to tell my parents, but they found out from my younger sister, Linda, and brother, David. Of course, I'd been the talk of Willow Glen that afternoon.

Even the kindergartners knew.

If the same thing happened to a kid today, he'd get a couple sessions with the school counselor, maybe even go into therapy to learn how to cope with the shame and humiliation. Xanax might be prescribed. But in the 1960s, you were pretty much left to your own devices.

Thankfully, Mr. Caldwell was right … to a point. The teasing was pretty brutal for a day or two, but it gradually subsided. Eventually, a week went by without a single wisecrack – pardon the pun – and then two. Life went on, and I didn't have to move to Bolivia, after all.

By the time I got to high school, the incident was largely forgotten, or so I thought. In botany class one day, toward the end of my senior year, I was trying my hardest to flirt with Brenda Allard when Lloyd Everard, sitting a couple of seats in front of us, turned around.

"Hey, Gary," he said with a conspiratorial grin. "Remember in eighth grade, when you came into the gym with your jockstrap on and bent over to get a drink at the water fountain?"

"Yes, Lloyd," I said through gritted teeth. *I remember my most embare-ass-ing moment, and thanks so much for bringing it up.*

Brenda, a junior who had gone to a different grade school, apparently hadn't heard the story, so Lloyd eagerly recounted all the gory details. I screamed inside my head for him to stop, but I have to admit he was highly entertaining and quite obviously enjoying himself. By the time he finished his little soliloquy, five or six more kids were gathered around and I was slumped in my desk, emasculated, tingling with shame and mentally trying to squeeze into the cracks in the ceiling tiles.

Where was Mr. Caldwell when I needed him?

The passing years have healed the wound to the point where I thought writing this chapter would be painless, maybe even cathartic. I thought I could be the butt of my own joke, so to speak, that I could effortlessly reveal to the reader what I revealed to my eighth-grade classmates all those years ago.

I was wrong.

Please excuse me, as I am feeling a little sick to my stomach.

How much is a one-way ticket to Bolivia?

Chapter 12

THE BOOB TUBE

Come and listen to a story 'bout a man named Jed.

Say, or better yet sing, those words to anyone born in 1960 or earlier and you will instantly get this response:

"Poor mountaineer, barely kept his family fed."

They were the opening lines of the theme song from *The Beverly Hillbillies*, perhaps the catchiest jingle ever written for television. The half-hour show's premise – a mountain man striking oil and moving his family of simpletons to Beverly Hills, where hilarity ensued – wouldn't work today. But I would be remiss if I didn't point out that Elly Mae Clampett (Donna Douglas) in a button-down shirt works in any era.

TV was still a fairly new medium in the mid-1960s. When you wanted to change the channel, you did it manually by twisting a dial on the set, typically a twenty-four-inch screen (or smaller) imbedded in an enormous wooden console that doubled as furniture. There were no cables or satellite dishes, just an antenna on the roof that never seemed to be pointed in the right direction.

TVs were far from smart ... or even competent. Occasionally, the bulky picture tube would go out, and your favorite show would look like a January blizzard until a repairman came to your house and fixed it. That's right. TV repairmen, like doctors, actually made house calls in the '60s. Today, you'd just take out a second mortgage and buy a 75-inch, 4K UHD Smart LED with HDR. What do all those acronyms mean? Don't worry, the kid at Best Buy who didn't graduate high school can explain it. Pretty soon, they'll come up with a TV that can pet the dog and flush the toilet ... if they haven't already.

Households now typically have three or four TVs, with family members in different rooms watching different Netflix series. But back then no middle-class family had more than one television. Why would you need a second TV when there were only three channels? You couldn't run to your room and surf Amazon Prime or Hulu. You sat cross-legged on the floor and watched what your parents watched. After you did your homework at the kitchen table, of course.

Around 1965, the Woyaks, our next-door neighbors, bought the first color television on the block and invited us over to check out the newfangled technology. We sat transfixed, waiting for the NBC peacock to spread its feathers. Seeing it in "living color" (as opposed to "dead color") was transformative. It was a quantum leap, like going from eight-track tapes to iTunes.

Despite all the hardships we endured, for my money, the decade of the 1960s was the Golden Era of television. Let's take a walk down memory lane ...

Gilligan's Island (1964-67)

Ginger or Mary Ann?

It was the burning question among pubescent boys on playgrounds across America. Ginger Grant (Tina Louise), the sultry Hollywood starlet, or Mary Ann Summers (Dawn Wells), the perky farm girl? They were stranded, along with Gilligan, the Skipper, the Professor, Thurston Howell III and his wife, Lovey, on an "uncharted desert isle."

It was among the silliest of the '60s sitcoms, shot in Studio City, Los Angeles, on a parking lot filled with water and decorated with fake coconut trees. A laugh track added to the absurdity. The typecast passengers of the SS Minnow wore the same clean and pressed clothes for all 98 episodes. Which brings up another question: why was Ginger wearing a shimmery cocktail dress for a "three-hour tour?" Not that we minded.

The Professor was brilliant, inventing all kinds of gadgets to make life more comfortable on the island, but he couldn't figure out how to patch a hole in a boat? Oy vey.

Lost in Space (1965-68)

The first year or two of its prime-time run, this was cutting edge sci-fi. The Robinson family, which was supposed to colonize a distant planet, was thrown light years off course with a stowaway and a clunky, arm-waving robot ("Danger, Will Robinson") onboard. Initially, the story plots were good, even if the acting was wooden.

There was even some early (for television) sexual tension between Major Don West and Judy Robinson, daughter of the mission commander, who threw furtive glances at each other but never, as far as we knew, removed their clothes. How the heck was this Pollyanna group ever going to populate a planet?

The show was nominated for two Emmys, though toward the end of its run, stowaway Dr. Smith had evolved from sinister villain to sniveling wimp.

You just wanted to throw something at the TV.

In the final season, the Robinsons landed on a planet and were captured by

Tybo, a giant carrot who turned Dr. Smith into a stalk of celery. Not surprisingly, the series was put out of its misery after just one more episode. It had jumped the shark before jumping the shark was a thing.

The Wild, Wild West (1965-69)

The animated opening to the show was cool and so was the main character, James West (Robert Conrad) – part scientist, part Western action hero and 100 percent machismo, battling the forces of evil as an 1860s-era Secret Service agent.

This was a Friday night staple in the D'Amato household. We sat on the living room floor, drinking Pepsi out of 16-ounce bottles and eating Mrs. Howe's potato chips as we waited for West and sidekick Artemus Gordon (Ross Martin) to extricate themselves from yet another predicament.

It was one hour of escapism. For James and Artemus, and for us.

The Dick Van Dyke Show (1961-66)

The comedic genius of the late, great creator-producer Carl Reiner and actors Dick Van Dyke, Mary Tyler Moore, Morey Amsterdam and Rose Marie made for some of the best television of the '60s, or any other decade.

The series was well-written, it was funny, and it was wholesome family entertainment. There was no agenda, no political messages, no sex or car chases or body bags. Rob and Laura Petrie slept in separate twin beds, for crying out loud. Rob tripping on the sofa was as violent as it got.

Shot in black and white – what's that? your kids are asking – *The Dick Van Dyke Show* probably would bore Gen Zers to tears. Which, when you think about it, is truly unfortunate.

Bonanza (1959-73)

When I was about ten years old, my parents took us to a model home in a sprawling new subdivision in suburban Milwaukee for the sole purpose of meeting Dan Blocker, who was making an appearance on behalf of the builder.

Everyone in America – and I mean *everyone* – knew him as gentle giant Hoss Cartwright, one of widowed rancher Ben Cartwright's three sons. I'll never forget shaking hands with him, my stubby little fingers engulfed in Blocker's catcher's mitt of a hand.

I had bragging rights at Willow Glen Elementary for a good week. *Man, you met Hoss?* Cue the cool guitar theme music.

At 430 episodes, *Bonanza* was one of the longest-running Western TV series in history.

Star Trek (1966-69)

Considering it had a relatively short run, its impact on the science fiction genre can't be overstated. The show gave us a cultural icon in Dr. Spock (Leonard Nimoy), scary villains in the Klingons, the magnificent Starship Enterprise, and permission to let our imaginations run wild. It also gave us Lieutenant Uhura, the lovely Nichelle Nichols, but I digress.

More than five decades later, Trekkies who weren't yet born when Captain Kirk was barking staccato commands on the bridge still attend sci-fi conventions.

Like *Lost in Space*, which pretty much ran concurrently, *Star Trek*'s writers ran out of ideas after a couple of years. As Example A, I give you "The Trouble with Tribbles." YouTube it sometime.

Leave it to Beaver (1957-63)

No cast of characters better captured stereotypical American suburbia than did the Cleavers:

June, cooking dinner in a dress and pearls; Ward, the unquestioned head of the household, putting down the newspaper and his pipe just long enough to solve a familial problem with the right mix of sternness and empathy; son Theodore (Beaver) perpetually getting into trouble; and big brother, Wally, perpetually bailing him out.

The dialogue usually went something like this:

"Gee, Wally, I only did it on account of I didn't think we'd get caught."

"Beav, ya little goof. Now what are we gonna do?"

The show was in afternoon reruns by the time I turned ten, but I believe I memorized all 234 episodes.

The Twilight Zone (1959-64)

I don't know what was scarier: the thought-provoking sci-fi show or the fact that narrator Rod Serling had no upper lip.

The series, in which ordinary people found themselves in extraordinary situations, remains entertaining in reruns six decades later. My favorite episode was "Nightmare at 20,000 Feet," starring a young William Shatner. You did not want to get on an airplane after watching that one.

Serling's chill bump-inducing opening narration changed slightly in each of the five seasons the show aired. From season two (cue Serling's voice): *"You're traveling through another dimension, a dimension not only of sight and sound, but of mind. A journey into a wondrous land whose boundaries are that of imagination. That's the signpost up ahead. Your next stop, the Twilight Zone."*

Dozens of film and TV stars had starring roles or cameos – many before they hit it big – in it, including Robert Redford, Dennis Hopper, Robert Duvall, Don Rickles, Peter Falk, Charles Bronson, Lee Marvin, Jonathan Winters, Carol Burnett, Burt Reynolds, Ron Howard, Mickey Rooney, Telly Savalas and the future cast of *Star Trek:* Shatner, Leonard Nimoy, James Doohan and George Takei.

Here are some other of my favorite TV shows of that era:

The Andy Griffith Show (1960-68): In the history of television, has there been a more memorable character than Barney Fife? Don Knotts played the nervous nelly, do-good deputy sheriff to perfection. Ron Howard, who would go on to *Happy Days* and later directing fame, cut his teeth as Opie, the son of widower Sheriff Andy Taylor. Who among us boomers doesn't on occasion whistle the theme song? See? You're doing it now.

I Dream of Jeannie (1965-70): The show first aired when I was nine years old, and I didn't understand my dad's fascination with Barbara Eden. It ended when I was fourteen, and by then I did. Can you imagine a TV show today in which the woman calls the man "master?"

The Addams Family (1964-66) and The Munsters (1964-66): More campy than spooky (and altogether ooky), both shows poked fun at the horror genre with cornball humor. It's hard to top Fred Gwynne as big-hearted dufus Herman Munster or Jackie Coogan as Uncle Fester.

Batman (1966-68): *Whap! Kapow! Thwack!* The Caped Crusader and sidekick, Robin, battled evildoers in Gotham City. The colorful villains – Joker (Cesar Romero), Riddler (Frank Gorshin), Penguin (Burgess Meredith), and Catwoman (Eartha Kitt and Julie Newmar) – were outrageously overacted, the dialogue intentionally wooden, the fight scenes ridiculously staged. For a short while, it was the hottest thing on TV. As Robin would say, "Holy pile of poo, Batman!"

Rowan & Martin's Laugh-In: (1967-73): The series featured cutting edge sketch comedy that often strayed into political incorrectness, paving the way for shows such as *Saturday Night Live* and *In Living Color*. My father called it "garbage." I loved it. Laugh-In introduced us to Goldie Hawn, Arte Johnson, Lilly Tomlin, and Ruth Buzzi, among others. All together now: Sock it to me!

Get Smart (1965-70): A silly send-off on James Bond movies. Don Adams, as fumbling, bumbling super-spy Maxwell Smart, was the polar opposite of the sophisticated British Secret Service agent 007. Then again, Smart did introduce us to the shoe phone and one of the most oft-repeated phrases of the '60s: "Sorry about that, Chief."

Mr. Ed (1958-66): "A horse is a horse, of course, of course, and no one can talk to a horse, of course. That is, of course, unless the horse is the famous Mr. Ed." Okay, the theme song wasn't written by Dylan, but you just had to sing along. The crew reportedly smeared peanut butter inside the mouth of Mr. Ed (real name: Bamboo Harvester) to get him to move his lips.

Today, somebody would complain to PETA about animal cruelty.

My Three Sons (1960-72): Trivia question: Who played the saxophone theme music at the top of the show? Answer: Fred MacMurray, the movie star (*Double Indemnity* and a bunch of Disney flicks) who played widower Steve Douglas raising three sons with the help of cantankerous Uncle Charley. A lot of kids in America grew up with Chip, Robbie, and Ernie Douglas. Believe it or not, Jodie Foster appeared in six episodes and Dean Martin, James Stewart, and Martin Sheen were among those who had cameos.

Mission Impossible (1966-73): Long before Tom Cruise played Ethan Hunt in the Hollywood blockbusters, Peter Graves was James Phelps, head of a super-secret government agency, the IMF (Impossible Missions Force). The opening scenes in which the highly sensitive mission is revealed before "this tape will self-destruct in five seconds" had us on the edge of our seats.

The Monkees (1966-68): Cashing in on the enormous popularity of four lads from Liverpool, NBC aired a short-lived comedy series about a struggling Beatles-esque band. It lasted just two seasons and fifty-eight episodes, but against all odds, the band that was cobbled together from auditions – former jockey Davy Jones; actors Micky Dolenz and Peter Tork; and Michael Nesmith, the only true musician among the bunch – had lasting fame and produced several monster hits in the '60s.

Gomer Pyle: USMC (1964-69): I honestly thought the perpetually frustrated Sergeant Vince Carter, played perfectly by Frank Sutton – who actually served in the Army during World War II – was going to have a real-life stroke on set as he dealt with hapless rube Gomer Pyle, played equally perfectly by Jim Nabors. This sitcom was so typical of the '60s – harmless, goofy, and innocent fare.

The Flintstones (1960-66) and The Jetsons (1962-63): William Hanna and Joseph Barbera created both series, giving us memorable cartoon characters Fred Flintstone, Barney Rubble, and George Jetson. Just as *The Flintstones* was inspired by *The Honeymooners*, *The Jetsons* was inspired by *The Dick Van Dyke Show*. The great Mel Blanc voiced Barney in *The Flintstones* and Cosmo Spacely in *The Jetsons*.

Hogan's Heroes (1965-71): Colonel Hogan (Bob Crane) and a ragtag group of inmates at a World War II POW camp conduct an espionage campaign right under the noses of the incompetent Colonel Klink and the bumbling Sergeant Schultz. Werner Klemperer (Klink) and John Banner (Schultz) were Jewish and immigrated to the United States after fleeing the Nazi regime. Klemperer reportedly agreed to play Klink only after being assured that the Nazi would be portrayed as a buffoon.

Green Acres (1965-71): Hey, it worked for *The Beverly Hillbillies,* so why not try it in reverse? Wealthy Manhattan attorney Oliver Wendell Douglas (Eddie Albert) flees the big city with his socialite Hungarian wife Lisa (Eva Gabor). They buy a run-down farm from a con man, Mr. Haney, and spend 170 episodes trying to adjust to the simpler life in Hooterville. Only in the '60s could a pig (Arnold Ziffel) have a recurring role.

Combat (1962-67): After a series of movies in the 1950s that glorified soldiers in World War II (and often the war itself), *Combat* provided a grittier, more realistic look at a weary and battle-hardened American infantry squad as it fought its way across Europe. Every kid on my block wanted to be squad leader Sergeant Saunders (Vic Morrow).

The Rifleman (1958-63): The first primetime TV series to feature a single parent as the main character – Chuck Connors as Lucas McCain – *The Rifleman* was a trailblazer in other ways. Developed by legendary director Sam Peckinpah, it was one of the first American TV series shown in Russia. Soviet leader Leonid Brezhnev was said to be a gushing fan and requested a meeting with Connors during Brezhnev's historic visit to the United States in the early 1970s.

The Man from U.N.C.L.E. (1964-68): Napoleon Solo (Robert Vaughn) and Illya Kuryakin (David McCallum), top agents for the United Network Command for Law and Enforcement, fight the forces of evil in another Bond rip-off. Their main adversary was T.H.R.U.S.H. (the Technological Hierarchy for the Removal of Undesirables and the Subjugation of Humanity). This series was H.E.A.T. (Highly Entertaining Action Television).

My Favorite Martian (1963-66): Computer-generated imagery in movies today make the antennae that extended out of Uncle Martin's head look like something from a fifth-grade science class. Heck, even back then they looked like something from a fifth-grade science class.

Bewitched (1964-72): This was one of my mom's favorites, partly because she claimed to be distantly related to star Elizabeth Montgomery, the nose-wiggling witch Samantha Stevens. Agnes Moorehead was great as Endora, Sam's mother and a perpetual thorn in the side of poor Darrin, Sam's whiny witch-pecked husband.

Chapter 13

THE THREE-YARD RUN

One of my earliest childhood memories is that of my father holding my hand and walking me across the street, when our family lived on Morgan Avenue on the south side of Milwaukee, and pointing to the football team practicing on the field at what is now St. Thomas More High School.

"Those are the Los Angeles Rams," he said as I peered through the cyclone fence.

Before you laugh, know that the National Football League then wasn't the multibillion-dollar, slickly marketed corporate entity that it is today, and it's entirely possible that the Rams could have practiced on a high school field. Decades later, out of curiosity, I looked it up: on November 20, 1960, the Rams beat the Green Bay Packers, 33-31, at County Stadium in Milwaukee.

The timing matches up.

The Packers would win NFL titles under Coach Vince Lombardi in 1961, '62, '65, '66 and '67. My dad, who had played running back for his Army post team, was a fanatic, pounding the arms of his chair in excitement as we watched Bart Starr and Ray Nitschke lead the Pack on all those autumn Sundays. One of the few times I saw him cry was when Starr scored the winning touchdown in the "Ice Bowl," the 1967 NFL Championship Game played in sub-freezing temperatures at Green Bay's Lambeau Field.

Many years later, as a sportswriter for the *Milwaukee Journal Sentinel,* I would cover dozens of Packers games, including their appearances in Super Bowls XXXI, XXXII and XLV.

It was clear from early on that football was going to be an important part of my life, which meant I would suit up for the mighty Mariners of St. Francis High School.

Alas, there were three problems. First, at the start of my freshman year, I tipped the scales at a less-than-robust 114 pounds. Second, in football, you get hit. Third, wanting to impress my dad, I signed up to be a running back, and running backs get hit a lot.

I was not a big fan of getting hit, and I suffered from a profound lack of self-confidence. In football, that is not a winning combination. I was the most tentative, timid kid on the field. It was hard enough being a first-semester freshman in high school without dreading football practice at the end of the day.

In a drill during one of our early practices, our coaches, Mr. Joncas and Mr. Guckenberger, set up cones in a line, staggered about five feet apart. They represented "holes" in the offensive line. The running backs lined up, took a handoff from the quarterback and had to pick a hole and run through it. On the other side, a defender waited to make the tackle.

On my first turn, I took the handoff and immediately made a sharp cut between the first two cones. The one thing I had going for me was that I was fairly fast. The defender waiting for me, my grade school pal Henry Brazil, completely whiffed. He didn't lay a hand on me.

I was pleased with myself, but mostly relieved that I hadn't gotten hit.

Then I heard a sharp whistle.

"What the hell was *that*?" came the booming voice of Dewey Schiele. Mr. Schiele was the varsity head coach, and I'd have rather faced Linda Blair in *The Exorcist* than his withering stare. From thirty yards away, he'd been absently watching the drill, which was meant to test a running back's ability to take a hit and fight for extra yards. I thought I'd done my job by running to daylight. After all, wasn't the goal *not* to get tackled?

Mr. Schiele looked at it another way. He thought I'd cheated the drill.

"Ligocki!" he shouted. "Get over here!"

Chris Ligocki came sprinting over. Starting defensive end on the varsity.

Six feet, five inches. Two hundred twenty pounds. Mean as a rattlesnake.

"Run it again!" Coach Schiele bellowed, then glared at me, nostrils flaring. He pointed at the middle two cones and said, "You'd better run right through here!"

I saw Ligocki grinning behind his facemask.

I swallowed hard and took the handoff, and when I made my cut through the middle two cones as instructed, Ligocki was waiting. He literally picked me up off the ground, folded me in half in his arms, and speared me helmet first into the turf.

Satisfied that I'd been taught a lesson, Schiele snarled and walked away.

It was a miracle I made it through the first week of practice. But as we started learning and running plays, I noticed I was the second-string halfback, behind only Jeff Jankowski. There were a couple more running backs behind me. Apparently, the coaches saw a little something in me that I hadn't seen in myself.

One day, we practiced against the junior varsity. The coaches had Mike McKeon, the jayvee quarterback, run our freshman plays. In the huddle, McKeon called "29 Jet Go," which was a pitch to me. Lined up to the left of the quarterback, I would run laterally to my left after the snap, take the pitchout and swing up field around the defensive end.

The play somehow worked to perfection. When I turned up field, I saw nothing but daylight. One of the jayvee linebackers, Mario Ramos, took a bad angle, and I beat him to the corner. A defensive back gave chase, but I was gone. The coaches blew the whistle after I had run about forty yards and shouted words of praise and encouragement to me, while chastising the jayvee defense.

Maybe I could do this, after all.

Back in the huddle, McKeon called the next play: "29 Jet Go."

I looked at him quizzically. We ran the play, and this time I gained three or four yards before two defenders crashed into me. Still a positive result.

Back to the huddle. McKeon was grinning now. "29 Jet Go," he said. Those were his buddies on the jayvee defense. He was trying to get me killed.

I took the pitch and immediately was met in the backfield by Ramos, undoubtedly stinging from the coaches' criticism. When I staggered to my feet, I was looking out the earhole of my helmet.

Gradually, though, my confidence grew. I started losing my fear of contact. I was the only kid on the freshman team who could long-snap the ball reasonably well, so when the games started, I was the snapper for extra points and field goals. That's right: a 114-pound center.

After three or four games, though, I still hadn't played a single down on offense. Then, during a scoreless tie against Greenfield, Joncas and Guckenberger became upset with Jankowski's effort. Near the end of the first half, Guckenberger turned to me and said, "Get ready, Dee-Amato. You're starting the second half."

We took the opening kick, and I trotted out with the offense, my stomach churning. The coaches wanted to see what I could do and wasted no time calling my number. Russ Szukalski, our quarterback, called "23 Dive," the simplest play in our playbook. I was to take the handoff and run straight ahead through the "3" hole, between the left guard and left tackle. If properly executed, this play would gain a few yards. It was not designed to be a big hitter.

Szukalski shoved the ball into my stomach and, wonder of wonders, the hole opened wide enough to drive a truck through it. The guard and tackle had executed their blocks to perfection. If a linebacker or safety were lurking, I didn't see him. There was nothing but grass between me and the goalposts, some seventy yards away.

I was going to score a touchdown on my first-ever carry!

A couple of yards later, however, I was flat on my face. My cleat had caught in the lumpy dirt passing as turf, and I'd stumbled to the ground. At least two seconds passed before a defender jumped on my back. To this day, there's no doubt in my mind I would have scored, perhaps even untouched.

On second down, Szukalski called my favorite play: "29 Jet Go." I peeled left on the snap, but he pitched the ball behind me, and I never had a chance to catch it. I ran back and fell on the loose ball and then was swarmed under by defenders.

After an incomplete pass on third down, Jankowski was back in the lineup, and I was back on the bench.

The next week in practice, I broke my thumb and was out for the season.

I went out for football again as a sophomore, but didn't play much. I'm sure my father was disappointed when I didn't go out for the team as a junior or senior, though he never said a word about it. I sat in the stands those last two years and watched my friends, part of me wishing I were still out there, but mostly glad to be done with it.

All these years later, though, I can still see that hole opening up. In my dreams, I stay on my feet and run to daylight, defenders sprawled in my wake as I cross the goal line.

Would my life have changed in ways big or small had I scored a touchdown on that crisp October afternoon in 1970? Would it have helped me become a popular jock instead of merely the kid who longed to be one? Would it have helped erase the gnawing feeling over the years that I somehow let my father down? These things are impossible to know. I had arrived at an intersection of possible destinies. My cleat stuck in the ground, I tripped and fell. And that was that.

And so, a long time ago, I gained three yards and was "credited" with a fumble and recovery on my only two official carries as a high school running back. On a planet with nearly eight billion people, nobody remembers but me.

Life is filled with these fleeting moments, important for reasons clear only to those who hold onto them. I guess that's the definition of nostalgia.

Chapter 14

THE DEER HUNTER

The deer hunt is a rite of passage in Wisconsin, when fathers and sons who sat around all fall watching football and drinking beer become, for one week, great hunter-gatherers. Like generations before them, they head to the north woods in their SUVs, fortify themselves along the way at bars in no-stoplight towns, rent cabins with cable TV, and play poker.

Some of them, when they're not too hung over, actually go out in the woods in search of the elusive white-tailed deer.

Ours was not a hunting family. The only things I hunted growing up were butterflies, tadpoles, and honeybees. When we needed food, we didn't go out and shoot a squirrel or rabbit. We drove six blocks to the A&P and filled our grocery cart.

But my father worked in a factory where men were men, hardened by years of assembly line work and the occasional all-nighter in the corner tap. Dad didn't own a gun, but every fall he borrowed one from a friend and went deer hunting with his buddies. He never bagged a deer – for all I know, he never even fired the gun – and usually arrived home disheveled and exhausted, whereupon he slept for eighteen consecutive hours. I figured deer hunting was hard work.

Still, what kid doesn't want to join his father on a deer hunt? It's the ultimate guy thing, bigger even than wrenching on a car or having a catch in the backyard. I had this romantic notion of moving stealthily through the woods for hours, coming across a majestic twelve-point buck in the clearing ahead, and making the perfect kill shot, all with my dad at my side. It doesn't get any better than that.

When I was sixteen, my dad asked me if I wanted join him and three of his buddies. I couldn't say yes fast enough. One of his friends had an extra rifle and let me borrow it. I'd never held a gun, let alone shot one, and was given a crash course in hunter safety: Never point a loaded gun at anyone; never pull the trigger unless you know what you're shooting at. Got it? OK, let's get started.

After we parked our cars on a gravel road, we hiked about a half-mile to our rented cabin, the men telling bawdy jokes and cussing like sailors. This was going to be fun. Our ramshackle cabin was small, cozy, and warm. One of the men went into town and came back with pizzas, and we stayed up past midnight, playing cards and talking guy stuff.

My dad shook me awake the next morning. It was five o'clock and still dark when we headed into the woods. A fresh blanket of snow had fallen overnight. I could see my breath in the cold, still air. No one spoke as we trudged along. After about thirty minutes, we split into two groups: my dad's buddies went to a ridgetop and would drive any deer down toward us. My dad and I posted behind trees and waited.

After a while, we could hear the men in the distance, making noise intentionally. Suddenly, I heard crashing in the underbrush, and a trophy buck bounded into view. I'd never seen such a magnificent animal, outside of the lions and tigers at the Milwaukee County Zoo. The buck stopped no more than thirty yards from me.

I glanced at my dad and he nodded. He wanted me to take the shot. Slowly, I raised the gun and disengaged the safety. The buck was standing with his flank exposed to me. Even I couldn't miss this shot. It would be like hitting the broad side of a barn.

I could feel my heart pumping in my chest as I pointed the gun. All I had to do now was pull the trigger. The buck, having run a half-mile or so, was making a godawful noise, a rasping, snorting sound, as it tried to catch its breath. I could see its sides heaving and plumes of steam coming from its nose.

I don't know how long I stood there. Ten seconds maybe, but it felt like an hour. I could not pull the trigger. This beautiful creature had done nothing to deserve death, and especially not at my hand. Perhaps subconsciously, I moved my foot and my boot made a squishing sound in the mud. The buck looked straight at me, and in that one last split-second, I could have gotten off a shot. But by then, my finger no longer was on the trigger.

Then it was gone, crashing through the underbrush.

When we met back up with my dad's buddies, they said they'd seen a buck and thought they'd driven it toward us. Did we see it?

Yes, my dad said, but it was too far away. We didn't have a good shot. Silently, I thanked him for covering for me. And in that moment, I realized we had something else in common. My dad was not a killer of deer. He wouldn't have taken the shot, either.

The rest of the hunt was uneventful. We burned the midnight oil in the cabin, playing cards and telling jokes. We went back out into the woods, but I never saw another deer. Thank God.

It was the first and last time I went deer hunting. I'd experienced it, and it wasn't for me. I have nothing at all against the deer hunt. It's a deep-rooted tradition in Wisconsin and is necessary to cull the herd. It's important to the state's economy, too. Hundreds of businesses "up north" rely on the annual influx of hunters and the money they spend to carry them through the winter.

Generations of fathers and sons have bonded over the shared experience, and generations to come will do the same.

A few years later, when my brother David turned sixteen, he went on his first deer hunt. He actually shot a spike buck and had the small antlers mounted. He regaled me with the story of how he shot it as it ran away from him, and I admit to having had pangs of envy.

Funny thing is, he never again went hunting. My dad stopped going, too, having never bagged a single deer in all those years. I always wondered how many shots he'd turned down.

My best memory of my only deer hunt is looking at my dad as he told his buddies that we were too far away from that buck to take a shot and understanding in that moment how much he loved me.

APPENDIX

POP CULTURE IN THE 1960s

TOP SONGS

(As determined by Billboard magazine)

	Song	Artist	Year
1.	The Twist	Chubby Checker	1960
2.	Hey Jude	The Beatles	1968
3.	The Theme From "A Summer Place"	Percy Faith and His Orchestra	1960
4.	Tossin' And Turnin'	Bobby Lewis	1961
5.	I Want To Hold Your Hand	The Beatles	1964
6.	I'm A Believer	The Monkees	1966
7.	Aquarius/Let The Sunshine In	The 5th Dimension	1969
8.	Sugar, Sugar	The Archies	1969
9.	I Heard It Through The Grapevine	Marvin Gaye	1968
10.	Are You Lonesome Tonight?	Elvis Presley and The Jordanaires	1960

TOP TELEVISION PROGRAMS

(As measured by Nielsen Media Research)

Season	Program	Network	Rating*
1960-'61	Gunsmoke	CBS	37.3
1961-'62	Wagon Train	NBC	32.1
1962-'63	The Beverly Hillbillies	CBS	36.0
1963-'64	The Beverly Hillbillies	CBS	39.1
1964-'65	Bonanza	NBC	36.3
1965-'66	Bonanza	NBC	31.8
1966-'67	Bonanza	NBC	29.1
1967-'68	The Andy Griffith Show	CBS	27.6
1968-'69	Rowan & Martin's Laugh-In	NBC	31.8
1969-'70	Rowan & Martin's Laugh-In	NBC	26.3

* Rating is percent of TV households tuned to a particular program.

TOP-GROSSING MOVIES

(As determined by Box Office Report)
Includes distributor and revenue (in millions)

1960

1. Swiss Family Robinson	Disney	$20.178
2. Psycho	Paramount/	$11.200
Universal		

1961

1. 101 Dalmations	Disney	$68.648
2. West Side Story	United Artists	$19.646

1962

1. Lawrence of Arabia	Columbia	$20.310
2. The Longest Day	Fox	$17.600

1963

1. Cleopatra	Fox	$26.000
2. How the West Was Won	Cinerama/MGM	$20.933

1964

1. Mary Poppins	Disney	$45.000
2. My Fair Lady	Warner Brothers	$34.000

1965

The Sound of Music	Fox	$79.975
1. Doctor Zhivago	MGM	$60.954

1966

1. Hawaii	United Artists	$15.533
2. The Bible: In the Beginning…	Fox	$15.000

1967

1. The Jungle Book	Disney	$60.964
2. The Graduate	Embassy/	$44.091
	United Artists	

1968

1. Funny Girl	Columbia	$26.325
2. 2001: A Space Odyssey	MGM	$25.522

1969

1. Butch Cassidy and the Sundance Kid	Fox	$45.953
2. The Love Bug	Disney	$23.150

WORLD SERIES CHAMPIONS

1960   Pittsburgh Pirates
1961   New York Yankees
1962   New York Yankees
1963   Los Angeles Dodgers
1964   St. Louis Cardinals
1965   Los Angeles Dodgers
1966   Baltimore Orioles
1967   St. Louis Cardinals
1968   Detroit Tigers
1969   New York Mets

NFL CHAMPIONS

1960   Philadelphia Eagles
1961   Green Bay Packers
1962   Green Bay Packers
1963   Chicago Bears
1964   Cleveland Browns
1965   Green Bay Packers
1966   Green Bay Packers (won Super Bowl I)
1967   Green Bay Packers (won Super Bowl II)
1968   New York Jets (won Super Bowl Bowl III)
1969   1969 Kansas City Chiefs (won Super Bowl IV)

WORLD EVENTS

1960
Democrat John F. Kennedy wins the U.S. Presidential Election, defeating Republican Richard M. Nixon
The Organization of Petroleum Exporting Countries (OPEC) is created
The United States sends 3,500 troops to Vietnam
1961
Soviet Cosmonaut Yuri Gagarin becomes the first person in outer space
Construction of the Berlin Wall begins
The Bay of Pigs is an unsuccessful U.S.-backed operation to overthrow Fidel Castro of Cuba
The Peace Corps is created
1962
The Cuban Missile Crisis has the world on edge
The Beatles release their first single, "Love Me Do," in the United Kingdom

Sam Walton opens the first Walmart Discount City store in Rogers, Arkansas
1963
President John F. Kennedy is assassinated by Lee Harvey Oswald in Dallas

U.S. civil rights leader Dr. Martin Luther King, Jr. gives his famous "I Have a Dream" speech in Washington, D.C.

The United States begins to use ZIP codes
1964
President Lyndon B. Johnson signs the Civil Rights Act of 1964 into law

The Ford Motor Company begins to produce and sell the Mustang

Sidney Poitier becomes the first Black actor to win the Academy Award for best actor
1965
The Vietnam War escalates, and opposition to it begins to mount in the form of anti-war protests

Mary Quant designs the miniskirt in London, and it becomes a fashion craze

The Voting Rights Act is signed into law by President Lyndon B. Johnson
1966
Indira Gandhi becomes the prime minister of India

The first episode of the popular television program *Star Trek* airs

The Soviet Union's unmanned Luna 9 spacecraft lands on the surface of the moon
1967
The Green Bay Packers beat the Kansas City Chiefs in the first Super Bowl

The first issue of *Rolling Stone* magazine is published

The 25th Amendment to the U.S. Constitution, which clarifies issues related to presidential succession and disability, is ratified

South African doctor Christiaan Barnard completes the first human-to-human heart transplant operation
1968
Civil rights leader Dr. Martin Luther King, Jr. is assassinated by James Earl Ray

The first unmanned Apollo mission, Apollo 7, is launched by NASA

Egypt's Aswan Dam is completed

The Civil Rights Law of 1968 is signed into law by President Lyndon B. Johnson
1969
Neil Armstrong and Buzz Aldrin become the first men to walk on the moon during NASA's Apollo 11 mission

The Woodstock Music & Art Fair takes place in New York and features acts such as Janis Joplin, Jimi Hendrix, Jefferson Airplane, and The Who

Gary D'Amato

The popular children's television program, *Sesame Street*, debuts
ARPANET, predecessor of the Internet, relays its first communications between Stanford University and UCLA

ABOUT THE AUTHOR

Gary D'Amato spent more than forty years as a sportswriter, the last twenty-eight at the *Milwaukee Journal Sentinel.* His assignments included eleven Olympic Games, twenty-six consecutive Masters Tournaments and three Super Bowls. He is a three-time Wisconsin sportswriter of the year, and in 2017 was inducted into the Wisconsin Golf Hall of Fame. D'Amato's writing has been honored by the Associated Press Sports Editors, Milwaukee Press Club, Wisconsin Newspaper Association and Golf Writers Association of America. He works for Killarney Golf Media, writing primarily for the website *Wisconsin. Golf*, and lives in Caledonia, Wisconsin, with his wife, Dee Dee.

www.ingramcontent.com/pod-product-compliance
Lightning Source LLC
Chambersburg PA
CBHW031231120626
46545CB00003B/1084